ROUTLEDGE LIBRARY EDITIONS: WW2

Volume 44

WHILE THE POPE KEPT SILENT

WHILE THE POPE KEPT SILENT

Assisi and the Nazi Occupation as told by Padre Rufino Niccacci

ALEXANDER RAMATI

LONDON AND NEW YORK

First published in 1978 by George Allen & Unwin Ltd

This edition first published in 2022
by Routledge
2 Park Square, Milton Park, Abingdon, Oxon OX14 4RN

and by Routledge
605 Third Avenue, New York, NY 10158

Routledge is an imprint of the Taylor & Francis Group, an informa business

© 1978 Alexander Ramati

All rights reserved. No part of this book may be reprinted or reproduced or utilised in any form or by any electronic, mechanical, or other means, now known or hereafter invented, including photocopying and recording, or in any information storage or retrieval system, without permission in writing from the publishers.

Trademark notice: Product or corporate names may be trademarks or registered trademarks, and are used only for identification and explanation without intent to infringe.

British Library Cataloguing in Publication Data
A catalogue record for this book is available from the British Library

ISBN: 978-1-03-201217-9 (Set)
ISBN: 978-1-00-319367-8 (Set) (ebk)
ISBN: 978-1-03-210903-9 (Volume 44) (hbk)
ISBN: 978-1-03-210904-6 (Volume 44) (pbk)
ISBN: 978-1-00-321763-3 (Volume 44) (ebk)

DOI: 10.4324/9781003217633

Publisher's Note
The publisher has gone to great lengths to ensure the quality of this reprint but points out that some imperfections in the original copies may be apparent.

Disclaimer
The publisher has made every effort to trace copyright holders and would welcome correspondence from those they have been unable to trace.

ALEXANDER RAMATI

While the Pope Kept Silent

Assisi and the Nazi Occupation

as told by Padre Rufino Niccacci

London
GEORGE ALLEN & UNWIN
Boston   Sydney

First published in Great Britain 1978

This book is copyright under the Berne Convention. All rights are reserved. Apart from any fair dealing for the purpose of private study, research, criticism or review, as permitted under the Copyright Act, 1956, no part of this publication may be reproduced, stored in a retrieval system, or transmitted, in any form or by any means, electronic, electrical, chemical, mechanical, optical, photocopying, recording or otherwise, without the prior permission of the copyright owner. Enquiries should be sent to the publishers at the undermentioned address:

GEORGE ALLEN & UNWIN LTD
40 Museum Street, London WC1A 1LU

© Alexander Ramati 1978

British Library Cataloguing in Publication Data

Ramati, Alexander
   While the Pope kept silent.
   1. World War, 1939-1945 — Jews — Rescue —
Italy — Assisi   2. Escapes
I. Title   II. Niccacci, Rufino
940.54'21   D810J4

ISBN 0-04-940054-1

Typeset in 11 on 12 point Garamond by
Red Lion Setters, Holborn, London
Printed in Great Britain by
Unwin Brothers Limited, Old Woking

Acknowledgements

The author wishes to express his deepest gratitude to the protagonists of this story, or their descendants, for providing him with invaluable assistance in recounting the events described in the book and in supplying him with documents, letters and in some cases diaries. Special thanks must be given, in addition to Padre Rufino Niccacci, to the late Bishop Giuseppe Nicolini, Professor Don Aldo Brunacci, Mother Giuseppina, Deborah and Paolo Jozsa, Hella Kropf, Nino Maionica, the late Giovanni Cardelli, Trento Brizi, Gemma Fortini, Dr Robert Müller, Violante Rossi, Professor Emanuele Testa, Matilde Vardi, Hanna Hirsh, Enrico Klugman and the late Margerita Viterbi and her daughters, Miriam and Graziella.

The author and publishers also wish to thank Moneta Nicola Industrie Grafiche, Milano for permission to redraw the map of Assisi which appears on the endpapers.

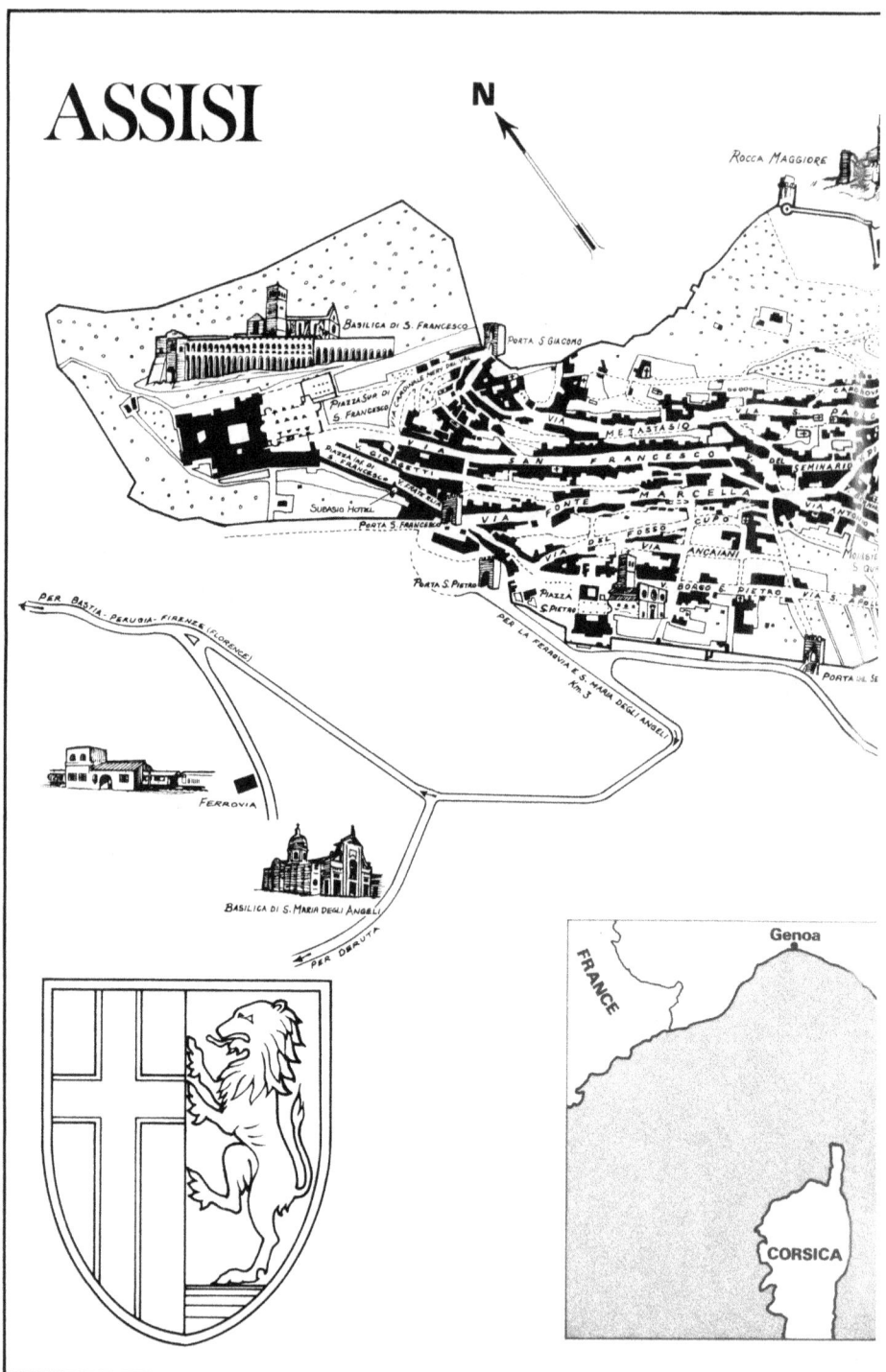

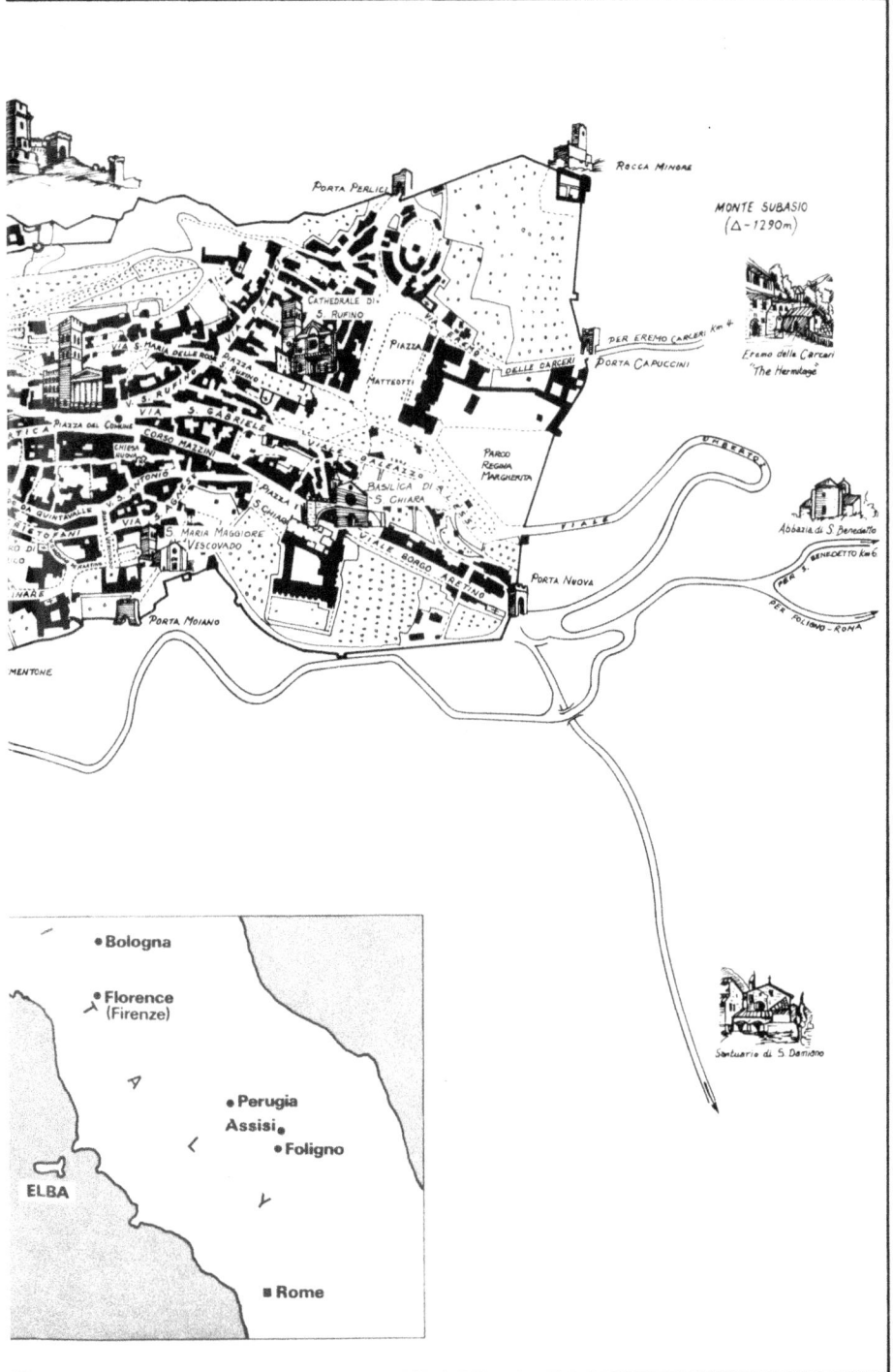

I

Rome fell to the Germans on 10 September 1943, and it was only on that day that the war really began for me, 120 kilometres to the north in the town of Assisi. Until then the Germans had not bothered us. They had come occasionally to visit our basilicas and cathedrals, smartly turned out and led by an education officer, usually a Catholic, who would tell them about St Francis and St Clare and talk about the famous painters who had painted frescoes in our churches. Even when they took Rome, the German troops stopped at the gates of the Vatican, so we could only hope that nothing would change for us and that they would simply continue to come to our holy city as tourists, which we would not really object to as they had always left large donations in our alms boxes.

Of course we had our Fascists throughout the war, but then we had had them ever since 1928, and they were all local citizens whom we knew well, good Catholics, who meant no harm to us. You could agree with their views or not, according to your conscience, as long as you did not express your objections out loud. Our Mayor, Avvocato Arnaldo Fortini, for example, had taken part in the Blackshirts' march on Rome in 1922, but he was also President of the International Society for Franciscan Studies and wrote many books about St Francis. And there was Signor Imperatore, in charge of the Fascist House, the Party's headquarters; Marshal Vivo, the commander of the Carabinieri; Pietro Coggoli, the pharmacist and councillor; and Ortensio Pagliacci, the city's chief accountant and head of the Blackshirts. They were the leaders and their views were shared by half of the city; which meant that two thousand people were for Mussolini, two thousand against him, and the rest were not involved in secular affairs. The rest were ourselves—one thousand monks, nuns and priests.

Events moved fast in the summer of 1943. On 25 July General Badoglio, with the help of Victor Emmanuel III, had ousted Mussolini. The Fascist House and the OVRA

(*Organizzazione Volontaria Repressione Antifascista*), the Fascist secret police, were disbanded, but Avvocato Fortini—he really was a good man—stayed on as Mayor. Six weeks later, Italy had signed an armistice with the Allies, the British had landed in Bari and the Americans at Salerno. In swift reaction, the troops of the Third Reich had stormed into Rome, overcoming our resistance and forcing the King and Badoglio to flee.

I was a young man of thirty-two then. For generations, the Niccaccis had lived in Deruta, a village famous for its pottery, ten kilometres from Assisi. We scraped a meagre living from a water-mill that had been in our family for so long that even our street was called after it; and there, at Via Molinella, I was born in 1911. When I graduated from the local elementary school and decided I would like to go on studying—well, there was then only one way for a poor Italian to get an education and that was to become a priest or a monk. I had always had a strong sense of religious vocation, having been brought up to adore St Francis, the patron saint of Italy, who lived, worked, performed miracles and was buried within two hours' walk of Deruta. I went to the high school in Todi, and then entered the seminary of San Damiano in Assisi. In 1942, after further studies and service in nearby monasteries, I returned to San Damiano as its Father Guardian and head of the very same seminary which I had attended as a student eight years earlier.

I was happy there. All I wanted was to serve God and St Francis, and the people of course, because that was what St Francis had preached. We owned a field, a vegetable garden and a vineyard, which I enjoyed. I have to admit that I am human and of course at the age of thirty-two I was even more human than now. I liked to eat well and drink well, and I was the only one among the monastery's fathers and brothers who smoked. To be honest, I was not even blind to a good pair of legs or a nice figure. I may have been a monk and a priest but I was also a peasant.

However, to return to my story, a few hours after I heard the news of the fall of Rome, the entire course of my life changed suddenly. I was to become a cheat and a liar—for a good cause, mind you, but nevertheless a sinner, although I am sure that I have long since made my peace with God and that He has forgiven my trespasses.

Those events occurred thirty-five years ago, but to me they seem as vivid as if they had happened yesterday. Perhaps because this was the most exciting and challenging year of my otherwise uneventful life.

It was around midnight and I was fast asleep on my coarse mattress of maize leaves, when I was awakened by a frantic call, 'Padre Guardiano! Padre Guardiano!' I sat up with a start and rubbed the sleep from my face. Above me, a candle in his hand, stood the tall, bearded Dutch Father Euralio Van Dyke. 'The sacristan of Santa Maria Maggiore is downstairs with an urgent message from the Bishop,' he said.

I leapt to my feet, slipped my brown habit over the undershirt in which I always slept, and hurriedly tied it with the knotted cord. With the help of Fra Euralio I found my sandals and dashed out of my cell, even before he was able to light the stairs for me.

In the closed courtyard of the multi-arched cloister, paved with pink flagstones, stood a young priest dressed in clerical black except for his stiff white Roman collar shining in the moonlight. 'The Lord Bishop wants to see you immediately,' the priest said.

Without a word, I started to go, but passing by the church I halted and gestured to the young man to wait a second. I entered, genuflected before the crucifix, dipped my hand in the holy water and crossed myself. I approached the altar and knelt next to Father Euralio, who, unlike other Franciscans, would get up at midnight to pray for his Nazi-occupied country and his bombed city of Rotterdam. After saying my *Miserere*, I buried my face in my hands, my thoughts wandering to the Bishop's summons. It was here that another man of Assisi had received his first call from Christ to restore the church and it was this church that the young man had rebuilt with his own hands, later to become Brother Francis and the creator of the First Order of the Friars Minor. It was not Christ who had called on me, only the Bishop, but I felt the strange excitement and anticipation of some important mission. I rose to my feet and hurried out through the large brick entrance yard, past the marble statue of St Clare, feeling, somewhat conceitedly, as if her raised hands were blessing me on my way to the Bishop.

The air smelled of rosemary and woodbine and the night was alive with the shrill chorus of cicadas as we made our way among low bushes and gnarled olive trees over the path that was a short cut to Assisi, one kilometre away. After a quarter of an hour's brisk walk, we passed through the wide arch of Porta Nuova into the walled, medieval town of rosy stone houses, now veiled in pale blue by the rays of the moon. Our sandals clattered, loud in the quiet night, as we crossed the huge paved Piazza Santa Chiara, past the Basilica where lay the body of St Clare. High above us I saw the Citadel of Rocca Maggiore and below us, at the foot of Monte Subasio, the immense Basilica of Santa Maria degli Angeli. We wound our way down crooked alleys, through arches under the houses, past shuttered windows adorned with flowerpots, wrought-iron hanging lamps and railed balconies. Occasionally, in a recessed doorway, a wan light glimmered at the shrine of a dusty Madonna, or a colourful relief of St Francis with a lamb under an olive tree brightened the façade of a house. One more flight of steps and we found ourselves on the Piazza del Vescovado, where behind the Romanesque Church of Santa Maria Maggiore, which used once to be the Cathedral of Assisi, stood the Bishop's Palace. The young sacristan went to his church and I paused in front of the palace gate to let my excitement die down a little before taking a deep breath and rapping the iron knocker.

After a while I saw behind the grille the small, frail figure of Emilia Cargol, the Bishop's niece. She opened the gate and led me upstairs to the reception room where the Bishop, dressed in a black cassock edged with red, a purple zucchetto on his head, sat in an armchair with hands crossed on his rotund belly. He was an amiable man of about sixty-five, with a pink, almost cherubic face and small alert eyes. Except for the throne on the podium, the big room looked startlingly austere, because Giuseppe Placido Nicolini had for thirty-seven years of his life been a Benedictine monk and his elevation to the episcopal throne in 1928 had not changed his ascetic way of life. He kept neither a secretary nor a valet, and only his widowed sister, Elena Cargol, and her daughter Emilia assisted him in running both his house and his office.

I knelt to make my obeisance and kissed his episcopal ring.

He helped me to rise and indicated that I should sit down. He looked at the curtained windows as if searching for appropriate words. Touching his pectoral cross, he turned to me. 'Cor ad cor loquitur,' he said. 'Heart speaks to heart. What I am going to say to you, Padre, must remain sub rosa, in strict secrecy between us.'

'Of course, Monsignore.'

'I want you to take care of some refugees who are now sleeping under my roof.'

'Refugees?' I asked, startled. 'What about Don Aldo Brunacci?' The Canon of the Cathedral of San Rufino was the head of the City Committee for Refugees who had fled from their war-ravaged villages and towns to Assisi in the hope that neither the Germans nor the Allies would bomb the city of our patron saint.

'They are not ordinary refugees,' the Bishop said. 'They are Jews who escaped from Rome today. There is a rabbi among them. I want you to take them to Cardinal Elia della Costa, the Archbishop of Florence.' From his sleeve he pulled out a letter. 'Read it,' he said. I opened the envelope. In the letter, signed by him, over his seal, Nicolini vouchsafed that the people I was to accompany on their journey were Christian pilgrims returning to their homes from Assisi. 'Della Costa will send them on to Genoa,' the Bishop explained, 'where Cardinal Pietro Boetto might manage to get them out on a neutral ship as he has done in the past with other Jews and political refugees.'

I hid the letter in my sleeve and raised my head. 'When do I go?' I asked, eagerly.

'Before dawn.' The plan was, Nicolini said, for our group to reach the Basilica of Santa Maria degli Angeli while it was still dark, and shortly before 6 a.m. to make a dash to the station, only a few hundred metres away, and go straight on to the train and thus avoid arousing suspicion.

The Bishop pointed to the couch and said his niece would wake me when it was time to leave. Then he smiled encouragingly and said he would get me a glass of wine. 'You'll sleep better,' he said. Modestly, I spread my hands in a half-hearted refusal, but I appreciated his gesture. Like me, the Bishop was also a peasant and while my family was grinding flour, his parents and ten brothers were squeezing grapes to make wine in the province of Trento. And a good wine at that. In his cellar Nicolini still had a few bottles left of the famous Santa Giustina for special guests. That night I was a special guest.

A few minutes later he returned with the glass of wine. I took a sip and smacked my lips. It was the best wine I had drunk since the beginning of the war. Then, warmed by the drink, I finally dared to ask: 'Monsignore, why did you choose *me* for this task?'

'Because', the Bishop said, 'you are the only friar in town who would not lose his head when questioned by the OVRA or the Gestapo. You are my uomo di fiducia, my man of trust.'

I felt deeply touched and honoured and I thanked the Lord Bishop for his confidence in me. When he retired to his chambers, Emilia brought sheets and blankets and made up a bed for me on the sofa.

When I was awakened, for the second time that night, a small group of people with suitcases and bags was already assembling in the room. Nicolini's sister, Elena, a tiny grey-haired woman, entered carrying a basket of food and handed it to one of the men. A moment later the Bishop made his entry, dressed in a nightgown and zucchetto, to wish us all a good and safe trip. I noticed that a man with a beard was clutching a suitcase against his chest. He thanked the Bishop for his hospitality, then asked him for one more favour. Opening the suitcase he took out a parchment scroll, topped by a silver crown, and asked Nicolini to hide it. It was a sacred Jewish Torah scroll, containing the first five books of the Old Testament, saved from a Roman synagogue, he explained. 'It's also holy for us,' the Bishop said, 'for it is part of our Scriptures, too.'

He promised to put the suitcase under his own bed to await the rabbi's return. If he failed to return, the rabbi added, he would be grateful if the Bishop would hand the Torah over to a Jewish community. A scroll had to be handwritten by scribes, and took some five years to complete. 'But why should you fail to return?' the Bishop asked. The rabbi told him all about the rumours he had heard of Auschwitz and Dachau and what they did there to the Jews. 'But you are in Italy,' the Bishop said. said. 'The Italians wouldn't stand for it. It couldn't happen here, not in the land of Dante, Manzoni and Petrarch.'

The rabbi's reply still rings in my ears. 'That's what the German Jews kept saying,' he said. 'It couldn't happen here— not in the land of Goethe, Schiller and Heine.' Then he reverently handed the scroll to the Bishop and led the group out of the room.

When they were all in the corridor, I approached my superior and kissed his ring. He looked searchingly into my face. 'I was born in Deruta,' I explained, trying to justify a tear or two in my eyes, 'and I have lived all of my thirty-two years around here. Though I know the Bible by heart, these are the very first Jews I have ever set my eyes on.'

Impulsively the Bishop put his arms around me. 'Go with God, my son,' he said. 'Benedicat te Omnipotens Deus.'

As our group entered the huge basilica, two befrocked, bearded men rose from a dark aisle and walked forward. One of them was the middle-aged, podgy Father Sebastian, who was in charge of the basilica. He had been informed of the plan and told me to pick up tickets in advance, and to include one more, for his companion Fra Felice. I shook hands with the young Franciscan. 'I'm so glad,' I said. 'It's better for two friars to lead the group. I'll be back in time for lauds.'

The deserted main street of the village of Santa Maria degli Angeli was still dark, but the stars had already begun to pale. The small station hall was almost empty, except for a peasant sprawled and snoring on a wooden bench and a woman sitting beside him with a cloth-covered basket on her knees. I asked for eleven tickets to Florence for the 6 a.m. rapido. The sleepy ticket-seller stared out into the hall. 'I'm leading a group of pilgrims,' I explained. 'They'll be here shortly.' The man began clicking the ticket machine and then told me that we had to change trains at Terontola.

As I left the station, the houses of Assisi perched on the mountainside were regaining their reddish hue in the early light of dawn.

In the Basilica of St Mary of the Angels, so called because in medieval times pilgrims claimed they heard the angels sing in the nearby woods, a procession of chanting Franciscan monks was already making its way to the choir. Father Sebastian stood in the door of the Chapel of Porziuncola, waiting for me. As I crossed the huge church, the rabbi rose from his bench and caught up with me. 'Padre Rufino!' he said. 'Could you kindly ask Father Sebastian if he could give us permission to conduct our service as well? You see, there are now ten of us, and whenever ten male Jews are present there can be a synagogue, even in a church.'

I looked at the man. 'You are nine,' I said, bewildered.

'Ten. Brother Felice is also a Jew.'

I threw a startled glance at Father Sebastian, who had overheard the conversation. He came over to me and pulled me towards the choir. He then explained that a few weeks ago a Brother Felice had died and been buried in the basilica's cemetery. A few days later a young Jew had asked for asylum; they had dressed him as a friar, made him grow a beard and had given him the necessary papers for the journey.

We took our places in the choir stalls and, together with other friars, began our lauds. As I was saying my paters and aves, I watched incredulously as the ten men put on black skullcaps, which looked exactly like the black zucchetti of the Franciscans. The Christians, twisting their rosary beads, were chanting their Angelus, and the Jews, swaying piously, were entreating God to protect them on their journey. At a quarter to six I got up and picked up a stack of breviaries from a pulpit. 'I'll return them,' I assured Father Sebastian. I dropped the books into a basket carried by one of the men. Father Sebastian accompanied us to the exit. Then he remained at the gate of the basilica, making the sign of the cross after the Jews who, led by two monks, one Christian and one Jewish, hurried to the station to catch the 6 a.m. rapido to Terontola.

A locomotive whistle could be heard in the distance. The station was empty and our timing was perfect. As the train drew to a halt, I led my group into an empty compartment, distributed the breviaries, and breathed more easily as, through an open window, I saw the station master bang a gong.

The train started to pull out of the station. Suddenly the door was flung open and a conductor appeared and asked for our tickets. Behind him I saw a man in civilian clothes, a grey borsalino low over his head, scrutinising the compartment—the two friars, the civilians, the breviaries in our hands and the rabbi whispering aloud: 'Santa Maria et omnes Sancti intercedant pro nobis ad Dominum.'[1]

The conductor punched the tickets and left with the OVRA man. Thankfully, I watched out of the window as the train began to move slowly over the bridge above the river Chiascio. As the white houses of Bastia came into view, it picked up speed. A quarter of an hour later it pulled into Perugia station. Some of the passengers left and new ones got on. The train started again, but a hundred metres further on it halted. On a platform, in front of a railway police building, I could see a detachment of Gestapo and a few civilians with black armbands. They jumped on to the train. As if by unspoken agreement, we all buried our heads in our breviaries.

Once more the door of our compartment was flung back. A German soldier barked something and the Italian interpreter translated his order. 'Your papers.' I handed the man our tickets. 'Not the tickets, papers!' the interpreter said. I passed the Bishop's letter to him. The Italian civilian read it and explained its content to the Gestapo man. The Nazi turned angrily to the rabbi. 'Erkennungskarte!' he snapped. 'Tessera di riconoscimento,' the Italian translated. 'Your identity card!' The old Jew started to fumble in his pocket, when suddenly the silence was pierced by the wail of an air-raid siren. The soldier momentarily froze, then he rushed to the window. The sky above the station reverberated with the roar of engines and the scream of dive-bombers. A huge explosion shattered the area. 'Raus!' the soldier shouted to his civilian companion. But the Italian interpreter had no need to be ordered out of the train, he was already running down the corridor. The German followed him. We heard the ack-ack of anti-aircraft fire. I saw a Gestapo officer anxiously signalling for the driver to pull the train out quickly. The wheels jarred against the rails and then began to turn, while the German soldiers and their Italian assistants made for the safety of the fields. I leaned out of the window, looked up and saw a pair of silver wings painted with the Union

---

[1] 'Holy Mary and all the Saints, please intercede for us with the Lord.'

Jack and an RAF emblem. The train by now was quickly picking up speed, leaving behind the bombed station of Perugia and the nearby Sant'Egidio aerodrome. As everyone sighed with relief, I kept my eyes on the sky, offering my deepest thanks to God and to the British.

II

After reporting on the successful completion of my mission, I did not see the Bishop for a while and imagined that this flight of the Jews had been an isolated case. Except for the South, Italy was now firmly in the hands of the Nazis, and after Mussolini's escape from an Allied prison and his formation of the Social Italian Republic, there were changes in Assisi. The Fascist House and the Blackshirts' brigades were re-established and the OVRA began searching houses and checking documents. As long as our own Fascists could keep proper control of the city, the Germans would not bother us, Mayor Fortini maintained. So we resigned ourselves to the new situation, and when people milled around the Piazza del Comune to exchange gossip or sip a brew of chicory roots in a cafe, they would look down at the columns of German tanks moving to the front along the main highway, relieved that they were bypassing our city.

Once a week, on Wednesdays, I myself would go to town to indulge in a game of checkers in the Cafe Minerva with Luigi Brizi, the local printer. He always wore a black borsalino which made him look somewhat taller than he really was. He had a good reason for wearing the black borsalino. His great-uncle, Eugenio Brizi, had been Mayor of Assisi, an associate of Garibaldi and Mazzini in the Risorgimento, the movement for Italian unity, and a man honoured with a city statue.

It was on one of these Wednesdays that I saw the Bishop's niece beckoning to me from across the piazza, so I quickly finished my cup of chicory, letting Brizi treat me to it as usual, and after surrendering my game to sweeten his disappointment I went over to Emilia. 'Monsignore wants to see you at once,' she whispered, and hurried off. I followed her down the tortuous alleys, convinced that as it was 29 September Nicolini was wishing to see me about arrangements for the Feast of St Francis, to be held in a few days' time.

The moment I entered his reception hall the Lord Bishop smiled broadly and extended his hand. He was flanked by the young, bespectacled Canon of San Rufino, Don Aldo Brunacci, and the elderly Father Michele Todde of the Basilica of St Francis.

'Padre Rufino,' he said, 'I have a new mission for you. Twenty Jews in Perugia are awaiting word from us.' It turned out that one of the group had come to Assisi and approached Padre Todde in the Basilica. Todde had run to Brunacci, Brunacci had taken him to the Bishop, and the Bishop sent for his uomo di fiducia—me. 'Of course we must hide them somewhere here,' the Bishop said, 'and prepare proper papers for them. The Germans are checking travellers much more intensively now.'

'What papers?' I asked.

'False identity cards, what else?' the Bishop said evenly, and then jovially clasped Don Aldo's arm. 'Some time ago I appointed you to be the Chairman of our Committee to Aid Refugees. I have now appointed Padre Rufino to the post of Chairman of our Committee to Aid Jews.'

That same evening the three taxis belonging to Geremia del Bianco stopped in front of the Monastery of San Quirico with the group of Jews who had escaped the Nazi round-up in Trieste. The Poor Clares ran a guest-house and, as far as Geremia knew, he had brought a group of Catholic refugees from Perugia. He had taken a side road, since the Germans did not like refugee transfers to interfere with their army movements.

I was waiting at the convent gate, greeting the arrivals as they filed past me, carrying their belongings through the paved courtyard and up the outer staircase. A tall young man with a black moustache paid the taxi drivers. He introduced himself to me as Giorgio Kropf and then we went upstairs. There the three externs, the out-sisters attending to the outside affairs of the convent, were already busy showing their guests to their rooms. Only the plump Suora Amata remained at the reception desk and she asked Giorgio to collect all the identity cards. The young man glanced at me, uneasily. 'No, Sister,' I said, 'no identity cards.'

'But this is the law. We must fill in the names in the guest book for the police to see.'

'No names,' I repeated.

'I think I'd better talk to the Mother Abbess.'

'Let *me* talk to the Mother Abbess,' I said. I was ushered into a parlour and sat on a stool in front of a double grille separating the cloister from the rest of the world. I heard the shutters behind the grille open and then the pale stern face of Mother Giuseppina appeared in the window. 'You wanted to see me, Padre Guardiano?'

'Yes, Mother...' I rubbed my mouth, searching for the right words to begin. Then I recalled the Bishop's approach to me on the very same subject, and I leaned forward. 'Reverend Mother,' I said, 'cor ad cor loquitur. What I'm going to say is sub rosa, just between us. Your sisters mustn't know about it. Those are not ordinary refugees, they are Jews.'

'Jews?' The Abbess clasped her palms. 'Poor people! I'm the only one here allowed to listen to the radio news, so I can tell the sisters for whom to offer prayers each day...'

'Good, then you know that the Jews are being persecuted, and that is why their names can't be put in the book.'

The Abbess rubbed the hard cloth of her white wimple reflectively. 'I see... but how can I keep this from the sisters?'

'Those are the Lord Bishop's orders.'

'I know. I'll swear them to secrecy. They've made many vows and kept them all. They will keep this one, too.' She got up. 'Anyway, it's time for the adoration and vespers and when their souls are reinforced by prayer, I will tell them.' And she lowered the lattice. Then the lattice immediately rattled up again and the Abbess called me back. 'I think I had better ask for your help, Padre. You have been Father Confessor to several of them. You had better explain to them about the Germans and the Fascists and the Jews. I've never been very good at politics.'

'All right,' I said. 'Shall I go to the church and wait there?'

'Yes, please.'

I made my way to the front and entered the small church of San Quirico, where the externs were lighting candles at the altar and putting flowers in front of the statues of the Madonna and St Clare. The sweet smell of incense filled my nostrils as I sat in the first pew, waiting. I heard the bells ring three times, the large, wide window opened behind the altar and I saw the distant faces of the nuns filing into the choir, chanting a psalm, then disappearing from my view as they knelt for the Angelus. I buried my face in my hands, rubbing it hard. I had preached many sermons, but the one facing me now was the most difficult. How was I going to explain all this to these women? Some of them had given their dowries to the Church forty years before and had shorn their hair to forgo any signs of earthly beauty. Ever since, they had walked barefoot, eaten only enough to survive, and spent most of their lives weeping over Christ's Passion. They lived only to die, to be buried behind the cloister's walls and to enter heaven, having deserved it by their earthly suffering and self-denial.

I raised my head and through the window of the choir I saw the monstrance, encasing the Host, which nuns were forbidden to touch, being lowered on a cord. I knew that the time had come for me to address my unseen audience. The sisters, now silent, were waiting for me to speak. They knew every step of the Via Dolorosa, but had never crossed the Via San Francesco; the Mount of Olives was nearer to them than Mount Subasio; Pilate and Herod were their enemies, but they had hardly heard of Hitler or Himmler, and some of them did not even know that the First World War had ended, let alone that a new one had already been raging for four years.

Then I heard the bells ring, urging me to begin. I can remember my exact words as if I had spoken them yesterday.

'Reverend Mother! Dear Sisters in Christ! You remember how our Saint, yours and mine, Brother Francis, repaired San Damiano with his own hands. When he had finished, the Lord appeared to him and told him it was not enough. He must, He said, not rebuild just one little church, but restore His entire Church. In those Dark Ages, God's Commandments were being broken and wars raged between nations, neighbouring cities and even between neighbouring families fighting for the control of those cities. And so that Brother Francis might set an example of brotherly love, God commanded him to find a leper, and embrace and kiss him. He ordered it, because the lepers were the poorest, the most wretched creatures, shunned, hated and chased from their homes.

'Once more, we live in the Dark Ages. The men and women who have come to you today to seek refuge and protection—they are the lepers of the modern world. They are Jews, who are being persecuted by the Germans and the Fascists, sent to concentration camps, then tortured and put to death.'

I paused and waited for the nuns' cries of horror and their frantic appeals for God's mercy to subside. Then I went on. 'We are God's sons and daughters, and we, brothers and sisters, have so much more to answer for than ordinary people. We must take those lepers into our arms, offer them our protection and hide them from their oppressors. We are the successors of St Francis and St Clare in this world which is once again filled with hatred, and we must follow their example in helping Our Lord to rebuild it with our brotherly love.' I mopped my brow and took a deep breath. 'It is the wish of our Lord Bishop and also of your Reverend Mother, that you, Poor Clares of San Quirico, now take an oath before this Holy Host, that you will shelter those people and never betray them.'

'Sia laudato Gesú Cristo! Praised be Jesus Christ!' I heard the supporting voice of Mother Abbess and then listened to her extracting the vow from her flock.

'May God bless you, Sisters,' I concluded. 'In the name of the Father and of the Son and of the Holy Ghost.' Then I got up, the bells behind me tolling for the end of vespers, and walked out of the church, with a happy smile on my face.

I went upstairs and knocked at one of the doors. 'Come in, Padre, please.' A small, dark-haired man, with an impressive Franz Josef moustache, showed me in. Through the door that opened on to another room, I saw three girls unpacking their suitcases. 'It's time we introduced ourselves. I'm Edward Gelb,' the man said, 'and this is my wife, Matilde.' A middle-aged attractive woman bowed her head. 'This is my father-in-law, Jacob Baruch.' I shook hands with a funny-looking, diminutive, bearded old man. 'And in the other room are our daughters, Deborah, Hella and Hanna. That's the entire Gelb family!'

'Where are you from?'

Edward Gelb waved his hand. 'Where do all Jews come from? From all over. The Baruchs originally came to Belgrade from Poland, the Gelbs are Yugoslavs. We all fled to Trieste from the Nazis eighteen months ago.'

'And the others? Do they all have an accent?' I asked, apprehensively.

'Giulio Kropf came to Trieste from Vienna after the First World War and he', Gelb shrugged, 'has an accent. Paolo Jozsa was born in Hungary, but has lived most of his life in Zagreb—so Pali, too, has an accent. But Giorgio himself doesn't. And his mother and her sister, the Cantonis, and her sister's husband, Maionica, are Italians. Why do you ask?'

'Because', I sighed, 'it's difficult enough as it is to try to pass you off as Italian refugees; it will be even more difficult if people hear you talk.'

Edward responded with a shrug of his shoulders. 'So we won't talk and we won't go out.'

'That's what I was going to suggest.'

'We didn't talk in the taxis. Giorgio made all the arrangements.'

'Good.'

There was a knock at the door and two more couples entered—Giulio Kropf, a small, bespectacled man, with his wife, Olga, plump and grey-haired and also wearing glasses. They were followed by Rita and Otto Maionica, both very tall and fine-looking. But before introductions could be made, Giorgio came in. 'Father, have you settled the problem of our registration?' he asked anxiously, the moment he crossed the threshold.

I grinned. 'Everything is settled and you have nothing to worry about. From now on, I am also going to be your Father Guardian.'

'We can hardly express our gratitude to you,' Otto Maionica began, when he was interrupted by Pali Jozsa, a handsome, dark, young man, with an engaging smile, who rushed into the room with a bottle of wine in his hand. 'We saved the bottle', he said in terrible Italian, 'for the occasion.'

'You'll stay and share a glass with us, won't you, Padre?' Gelb asked.

I pulled out a packet of cigarettes. 'I never refuse a glass of wine. A house-warming party, eh?'

'No, no,' old Baruch said. 'Tonight is the eve of our New Year. Rosh Hashana, 5704.'

I lit a cigarette and passed the packet round. 'I'll have to learn a little more about you Jews. Frankly, I know nothing.'

Old Baruch smiled and dug a small, well-thumbed book out of his pocket. 'This is all there is to know about our religion.'

I looked at it, then leafed through its pages. 'This is the Old Testament,' I said.

'That's it.'

I scratched my head. 'And nothing—nothing from the New?'

'No.'

'Just the Old?'

'That's right.'

Otto Maionica left the room and a moment later returned with a large book. He gave it to me. 'You may also want to read that,' he said. 'This is the history of the Italian Jews. You'll learn from it that all of them, just like us, the Maionicas and Cantonis, have always been part of Italy. Jewish soldiers fought and died for Garibaldi, Jewish bankers supported Cavour and Mazzini, and our scientists and writers made Italy's name famous all over the world.' I thanked him and promised to start reading the book immediately after the Feast of St Francis.

As we talked, Giorgio set glasses on the table and Pali uncorked the bottle. 'Just a moment,' Baruch said. 'Prayers first.' He opened his suitcase, pulled out skullcaps and passed them to all the men. As he got to me, he jovially waved me away. 'You don't need it, you already have one.'

'Wait, please!' I said. 'If we're going to celebrate the New Year, let's celebrate it properly!' and I dashed out of the room.

In the dining-hall, two distinguished old ladies, who, I learned later, were Giulietta Cantoni, Olga's and Rita's mother, and her friend Clara Weiss, were having a cup of fennel tea, talking about their vacation in Meran the previous summer which they had still managed to enjoy. Giulietta's granddaughter,

Gianna Maionica, a curly-haired little girl of ten, was admiring a poster featuring St Peter's Church, with a sign beneath: 'Visitate Roma—Città Eterna'. The externs were busy setting the tables for supper. At the sight of me charging into the room, Suora Amata turned from the linen cupboard and assured me that now they all understood my preoccupation and that I could rely on them completely.

'Good!' I turned to the others. 'Sister Alfonsina, go and dig out some bottles of wine from your cellar. I'm sure you have a couple left. You, Sister Beata, go and cut some flowers in your garden and fill the vases. And you,' I addressed the fourth extern, forgetting her name, 'go to the kitchen and make sure the food you serve is the best you have. You see, tonight is the eve of the Jewish New Year. Rosh Hashana, 5704.'

'I'll see that it is all done properly,' Suora Amata volunteered. And it was with immense pleasure and satisfaction that I watched the four nuns rush out of the room to help usher in a new Jewish year in the Catholic convent of San Quirico.

III

The Basilica of St Francis was full and the people who could not get into one of its two churches remained on the piazzas outside, listening to the voices of the choir. It was Sunday, 3 October, and it was the eve of the Feast of St Francis, the patron saint of Italy.

In the lower church, I was sitting in one of the first pews among other religious and lay dignitaries of the city—the church canons, the rectors of the seminaries, the abbots and father guardians, the Mayor and the members of the City Council. We were all watching the Lord Bishop, dressed in a resplendent white soutane, embellished with silk, and wearing the golden mitre, conducting the Rite of Transition from his throne by the High Altar. For it was at the very same hour

717 years ago that St Francis had died on the bare ground of Porziuncola.

The chorus of friars intoned 'O Sanctissima Anima', and from all the naves, all the altars and oratories of the basilica came the responses. The mournful chant of the brothers faded and the crowd knelt for silent prayer and meditation. Slowly, as dusk fell on the church, the friars' voices rose once more, 'Voce mea ad Dominum clamavi... With my voice I cried unto the Lord,' and David's lament, echoed by the congregation, reverberated through the arches, columns and vaults of the basilica.

Mayor Fortini, wearing all his royal and Vatican decorations, rose from his place, and when the chanting ended he approached the rail at the entrance to the crypt below the High Altar, lit a taper, and said in a loud voice:[1]

'Assisi, in the name of all the Italian communes, offers you, St Francis, oil for your lamp, as our votive offering. Since you became our Patron Saint,[2] Rome, Turin, Milan and Genoa have all had the honour of bringing their annual offering of oil to keep the light of vigil burning at the entrance to your tomb. The time has now come for your own beloved city of Assisi to express its infinite devotion to you and to ask for your protection of our beloved country, torn apart and once more ravaged by war. Let your lamp light our path, so that we may find our way, as you did, through peace and good will. Pax et Bonum!'

And as he spoke St Francis's message to mankind, the Mayor of Assisi lit the lamp at the tomb of the Saint.

Bishop Nicolini now rose from his throne, approached the altar and raised his hands. 'Dies Mortis—Dies Natalis,' he said, 'the day of death is the day of birth.' And, as the priests and brothers lit candles throughout the basilica, the sorrow over the Saint's death gave way to joy over his ascension to heaven. But as the Bishop was about to address the congregation, he stopped, for he heard a growing murmur of voices. We turned

---

[1] The text of his address is taken from his book: Arnaldo Fortini, *Quelli Che Vinceranno* (Those Who Will Win) (Del Romano Editore, Foligno, 1946), p. 184.

[2] Proclaimed by Pope Pius XII on 18 June 1939—thanks to the tireless efforts of Bishop Nicolini.

our heads towards the back of the church. There, in the middle of the aisle, between the last row of pews, stood a German lieutenant.

There was a hushed silence. The officer beckoned to one of the friars and whispered something to him. Father Todde, rushing to wave the German to a seat, met the friar half-way down the aisle. He received the message, flashed an angry look at the lieutenant, then sought out Mayor Fortini. The mayor rose from his seat. 'Now?' he asked, incredulously. 'At this very moment?!' Padre Todde nodded with a stifled sigh.

'How could they?' Bishop Nicolini stepped forward, ready to intervene, but Fortini had already begun to walk towards the German officer.

The lieutenant saluted. 'Arnaldo Fortini?' he asked. 'The Mayor of Assisi?'

'Yes?'

'Captain Stolmann wants to see you and Bishop Nicolini.'

'Who? Where is he?'

'Across the piazza. At his headquarters in the Hotel Subasio.'

Fortini nervously adjusted the glasses on his aquiline nose, turned to the Bishop and opened his hands in a gesture of complete bewilderment. 'I'm conducting a service now,' Nicolini said, indignantly. He scanned the first rows of pews and saw me. 'Padre Guardiano, go with the Mayor as my representative.'

I bowed obediently and followed Avvocato Fortini, while the Bishop pointedly began his address to the congregation. The moment Fortini and I stepped outside the church, we stopped. Right there, in the middle of the huge Lower Piazza, outlined by the light of candles held by the kneeling faithful, we saw the massive silhouette of a German tank, its long gun pointed at the basilica.

At the sight of us following the lieutenant, Signora Violante Rossi, the hotel owner, clasped her hands and rolled her eyes heavenwards. The lobby was filled with officers who drank schnapps and talked loudly, and it was hard to believe that the Germans had taken over the hotel and the city in a single hour while the town dignitaries were all gathered in the basilica. The lieutenant knocked at a room with a freshly nailed door-plate which read: 'Hauptmann Ernst Stolmann, Luftwaffe, Stadtkommissar—Commandante della Piazza.'

From behind the desk rose a Nordic-looking young man, with a powder-smooth face and pale blue eyes. The lieutenant immediately explained that I represented the Bishop who was conducting a service, then withdrew from the room. The captain waved us to two chairs facing him. 'Your town', he said in heavily accented Italian, 'has now fallen under the protection of the Third Reich. We have requisitioned the hotels Subasio and Windsor-Savoia, and, to help us keep order, a detachment of our military police has settled at the Giotto. We have no intention of intervening in your civic or religious affairs, providing the inhabitants do not interfere with our war effort.'

Fortini blinked. 'We have a good Fascist administration,' he began; 'our own police and the OVRA are very efficient...'

'Good,' Stolmann interrupted, 'then your administration will cooperate with us—for the sake of our common cause. Now...' The German opened the top drawer of his desk and pulled out a poster printed in two languages. 'This will be put up tonight in all public places.' He turned the poster towards us to read.

I saw 'ACHTUNG! ATTENZIONE!' in capital letters, and then the Mayor and I read the instructions given in Italian:

> All citizens must surrender their arms within 24 hours—under penalty of death.
>
> Night curfew must be observed from dusk to dawn. Anyone found out of doors at that time will be shot.
>
> Any person taking part in an act of sabotage, obstruction of military movement, or attack on German military personnel, will be shot on the spot.
>
> Reichsführer SS Heinrich Himmler.

When the Captain saw that we had finished reading, he turned to Fortini. 'Now, to ensure your town's observance of law and order, by tomorrow I want a list of twelve people picked from the most suspect elements—I'm sure your OVRA has such a list—whom we shall take into our custody as hostages. In the case of any armed attack on our soldiers, three of your hostages will be shot for every German life lost.'

Arnaldo Fortini looked at the captain as if not comprehending. 'Hostages?' he finally said. 'You want *me* to deliver Italian hostages to *you*?' With a dramatic gesture, he pointed at all the medals and decorations he was wearing for the Feast of St Francis, and told the officer about the march on Rome with Mussolini in 1922 in which he took part and about his rule of Assisi for the entire XXI[1] years of the New Imperial Fascist Era.

Stolmann shrugged. This was a very modest request, he said. For an act of sabotage committed by a Jew, the Germans shoot ten of them on the spot. 'I'm sure that after a little reflection', he concluded, 'you'll find it better that we hold some anti-Fascists responsible for the city's behaviour, rather than *you*.' He now turned to me and asked me to assure the Lord Bishop that the men under his command would respect our holy places, churches and monasteries. One out of three German soldiers was a Catholic, he pointed out, and many of them undoubtedly would participate in the holy procession the next day. He got up, walked us to the door and cordially shook our hands. And then, as an afterthought, he asked how many Jews there were in the town.

Not one, the Mayor answered. Not a single Jew had lived in Assisi throughout its entire history.

Once outside, as we were walking across the piazza back to the Basilica, the Mayor exploded. How naive he had been to believe that by re-establishing Fascist rule in the city he could keep the Germans out. Why, he struck his clenched fist against his palm in fury, why had the Germans not come to our city—to our country—as friendly allies instead of as ruthless occupiers? Oh, no, Mayor Fortini was not going to deliver Italian hostages to them! Because by tomorrow there would not be a Mayor Fortini.

And as we were mounting the steps of the Basilica of St Francis and could just hear the distant calm voice of our Lord Bishop, little Arnaldo Fortini straightened himself up, halted and informed me that tomorrow morning he was going to hand

---

[1] The Fascists spelled their reign in Roman numerals.

in his letter of resignation as Mayor of Assisi, a position which he had held proudly for over two decades.

IV

I will never know whether the Germans planned it that way or whether they had been infuriated by the Mayor's resignation and refusal to hand over the hostages. But barely an hour after the procession had ended, the first razzia in Assisi began.

At sunset on 4 October, the Sonderkommando from Bastia, Waffen SS from Foligno, and Gestapo men from Perugia converged from all sides, quickly set up road blocks, then moved in and barricaded all seven gates of the city, trapping the people behind its walls. Then, with perfect timing, coinciding with the start of the curfew, the trucks, laden with armed soldiers, silently wound their way through the deserted streets in the eerie glow of their dimmed headlights. They halted at the main piazzas for their rendezvous with the local German and Italian police who were patrolling the town. From there, mixed groups of soldiers and policemen fanned out through the medieval lanes and began their search for suspected partisans, anti-Fascists, for Italians avoiding the call-up and any Jews hiding from deportation. Black Volkswagens circled through the town, with German officers and OVRA men promising large rewards to anyone who informed on the enemies of the Third Reich and the Social Italian Republic,[1] and threatening death to those who failed to give information.

The stone houses were dark, their windows shuttered and doors locked, with people huddled together, listening to the thud of heavy boots and the brisk army orders, the pounding on doors and the rattle of rifle bolts.

[1] The Social Italian Republic, also called the Republic of Salo, was the new Fascist régime set up by Mussolini, after his escape, in the town of Salo on Lake Garda.

The moment I learned about the razzia, I rushed frantically back to the city and reached San Quirico shortly after the externs had given the news to the Mother Abbess, who had immediately gathered all the nuns in the choir to pray for St Clare's intercession. The Jews meanwhile, the Gelbs, the Kropfs, the Maionicas and the others who in the first days of October had followed them into hiding, sat in their rooms. Panic-stricken, they strained their ears for any sounds of distant voices or the rumble of vehicles breaking the night's silence. The old men donned their skullcaps and prayed, women wept quietly, young men made desperate plans to fight their way out if caught. When they learned I was in the reception room, they rushed to me as if I were the Messiah ready to save them. But I had no time to quell their fears as I was yelling at Suora Amata, 'Where the hell is the Mother Abbess?'

'In the choir, with the sisters, praying.'

'Good Heavens!' I exclaimed. 'Praying—at such a time? Lead me to her!'

'I can't interrupt her prayers.'

'Call her into the parlour, immediately!' I moved a step forward and the fat nun fled the room.

A moment later I was facing Mother Giuseppina across the grilled window. 'Open these doors, Mother!' I said, pointing at the wooden door, protected by a double grille, to which only the Abbess and a nun-doorkeeper had the keys.

'What? That's the cloister.'

'Do you think I don't know that? Get all the Jews in there.'

'Men? Men in the cloister? In a female cloister? You're out of your mind, Father! We have all taken a vow of seclusion.'

'Then break it!' I snapped.

The nun crossed herself. 'Never! Never in the seven hundred years, since Pope Innocent IV established our Order, has the Canonical Enclosure been broken. In the Papal Bull, St Clare in her own name, and in the name of her successors, promised obedience to the Pope and only the Pope can command me to break the vow.'

'In the same Article One of the Bull you're referring to, Mother, the Abbesses promised to obey St Francis's successors. I, as the Father Guardian of San Damiano, am giving you an order now.'

'You're a shrewd man, Father. I know that, we all know that... but you can't order me about. Only the Pope or his Cardinal in charge of the Franciscan Order could command me to let men into the cloister.'

'The Pope and the Cardinal are far away.'

'St Clare is near. She will protect us, protect us all. Didn't she manage to put the Saracens of Frederick II to flight in 1241? You'll see, the Germans won't even enter the convent.'

'Mother!' I became furious. 'It's a matter of life and death.'

'What is death,' the nun answered serenely, 'if not a step to real life?'

I clasped my hands in despair. 'Oh, God!' For a moment I was ready to explode, but I bit my lips to contain my rage and rushed out of the parlour. At the top of the stairs, I encountered Giorgio Kropf's pale face, his glazed eyes questioning me. 'That stubborn nun!' I scowled. 'What could you expect from women who shave their heads and pray all day! God, there is a time for prayer, but there is also a time for action. I'm going to get the Bishop.' And I ran down the steps and out of the gate, hurrying towards the Piazza del Vescovado.

Just as I reached the piazza, I heard a roar and an SS motorcyclist in helmet came to an abrupt halt by my side. 'Where do you think you're going, Padre?' he shouted in German, but I understood.

I glanced at the light machine-gun mounted on the handlebars. 'A sister,' I said in Italian, 'a nun—is very sick. She needs a priest.' As the German blinked, not understanding a word, I mimed what I had just said, showing the habit, imitating a dying person, pointing at the Bishop's Palace.

'Ah,' the SS man nodded. 'Das letzte Sakrament. Ich verstehe, ich bin selber katholisch.' And the Catholic soldier of the Third Reich waved me on.

'Thank you, St Clare,' I whispered, for a moment giving Mother Giuseppina her due. A few minutes later, I was knocking on the Bishop's gate until Elena Cargol opened and led me in.

Nicolini himself met me half-way up the stairs. 'What's the matter?' I reported the situation to him. The Bishop turned to his sister. 'My coat!' He grabbed it and pushed me forward. 'Come on!'

We rushed down the Via Giacomo di Martino, our hearts pounding from effort and fear. 'How did you get through to me?' Nicolini asked.

'I told a patrolling soldier that a nun was dying and wanted to see you.'

A sudden distant scream pierced the stillness of the night. 'I'm not guilty! I don't belong to the Resistance!' Then there was silence again. We walked on briskly and a moment later saw a truck in a side alley and a young boy being pushed into it, with his mother running after him, imploring the soldiers to let him go, because he was only seventeen and too young for the army.

'Hey, you!' The Bishop and I froze. An Italian policeman ran up to us, followed by a Gestapo man. 'It's curfew,' the policeman said, then, recognising Nicolini, he saluted. 'Monsignore,' he said more politely, 'the curfew is also for you.'

'A nun is dying,' the Lord Bishop of Assisi said, without batting an eyelid, 'and she wishes me to administer the last rites.'

'Oh, I'm sorry...' The policeman explained the matter to the Gestapo man and the latter waved me and the Bishop on.

Just at the entrance to San Quirico, I saw another patrol down the street, knocking at the gates of a Benedictine monastery. 'They do check the convents,' I said glumly.

'If only they had some false identity cards,' Nicolini sighed, climbing the staircase.

At the sight of the Bishop, Suora Amata rushed down a few steps, curtsied and kissed his ring. 'Oh, Monsignore! I'll tell Mother Abbess you're here.'

'Be quick, Sister. There's no time.' The Bishop burst into the parlour, with me close at his heels. A second later the window was opened and Mother Giuseppina appeared, lowering herself on to a stool, her palms entwined in her favourite, praying position. 'Break the Enclosure, Mother,' the Bishop said crisply. 'Let all the Jews in.'

'I need the Pope's order. Or the Cardinal's.' She glanced at me standing at the door.

'I'm the Pope's representative in this diocese and I'm carrying out the Pope's order,' Nicolini said.

The nun opened her mouth, then clicked it shut. 'I didn't know, Monsignore.' She grabbed his hand through the opening in the grille and made her obeisance.

'It's His Holiness's order to save human lives at any cost. And now, Mother, please move. The Germans are across the street, at the Benedictine monastery.'

Incredulously, Mother Giuseppina's crossed hands moved to her chin. 'They entered a monastery?'

'That's right. Hurry, please!'

Without a word, the Abbess beckoned to one of the nuns in an adjacent room of the cloister and told her to inform all the sisters of her decision. Then she approached the door, got her key, crossed herself, and first unlocked the wooden door, then the iron grilles protecting it. The Bishop and I exchanged a smile of relief. I immediately rushed into the guest-house, knocking at all the doors. 'Come quickly into hiding, all of you!'

Nobody needed to be told twice. Carrying their few belongings they hurried into the parlour of the convent. Mother Giuseppina stood in the open door, and whenever a refugee passed through into the cloister she made the sign of the cross and said, 'Sia laudato Gesú Cristo.' They all filed in, over thirty people—the Kropfs, the Gelbs and the Maionicas, the Provenzal family from Libya, the Jacobson family from Holland, and another branch of the Maionicas who had arrived only the day before and, though baptized, were still Jews under the racial laws of Germany and Italy. 'Where shall we put them all?' Suora Amata clasped her hands.

'In all the nuns' rooms,' the Bishop said. 'Even yours, Mother Abbess.' The Mother nodded, now eager to cooperate.

'I'm glad the Pontiff's orders came just in time,' I said quietly to the Bishop. No one heard us.

'The Pontiff, I am sure,' the Bishop answered evenly, 'would have given such orders if he were in my place.'

But just as the last refugee had passed into the cloister, we heard a vehicle coming to a halt outside on the street, the rumble of Italian and German voices and then the hard knocking of a rifle butt against the convent gate. The Bishop and I quickly rushed into the cloister. While Suora Amata went downstairs, Mother Giuseppina locked us all in, behind the double grille.

From below came the sound of a gate opening, and a brusque Italian question, 'Have you any refugees here?'

'There is no one in our guest-house at present,' Suora Amata answered.

'Let me see the guest book.' We heard the thud of boots mounting the stairs, then after a while came the same Italian voice saying that no, there were no guests registered in the guest-house, and a brisk German order in response, followed by quick steps and kicks on the doors as the Gestapo men checked the rooms.

Suddenly Mother Giuseppina unlocked the double grille and bolted across the parlour. 'How dare you!' we heard her indignant voice coming from the reception room. 'How dare you enter the monastery with arms and question us, the daughters of God?'

During the tense moment that ensued, the Bishop and I held our breath, our eyes glued on the cloister's double grille left open by Mother Giuseppina in her hurry. Then the noise of the soldiers being shooed away reached our ears, followed by the voice saying, 'I'm sorry, Mother. Please forgive us. Alles ist in Ordnung.' The soldiers' footsteps receded down the stairs. We walked out of the cloister and poked our heads into the corridor separating the parlour from the guest-house. Across it, through the door of the reception room, we saw the little figure of the Mother Abbess, her hand raised imperiously, waiting for the convent's gate to shut.

'Sia laudato Gesú Cristo,' she sighed, making the sign of the cross, probably in much the same way as St Clare had done after the retreating Saracens in 1241.

V

Shortly after the razzia, our monthly meeting of the International Society for Franciscan Studies took place in Arnaldo Fortini's villa. I always enjoyed the walk through the Upper City, past the Piazza of San Rufino—where the women washed their laundry in the ancient fountain, filled with water from a gargoyle—and then along the honey-tinted houses of the Via Santa Maria delle Rose, brightened with pots of geraniums hanging from the walls. At the end of the street stood the Villa Fortini, its gate open to lead visitors through a cypress-shaded alley up to the two-storeyed house, its verandas cloaked in blue wisteria.

Arnaldo Fortini and his small, greying wife, Emma, stood in the doorway, greeting the guests. But this time, after shaking my hand, the Avvocato took me aside and said he would like me to remain after the meeting to consult with me on some important and confidential matter. Their daughter, Gemma, led me and a few other people who had just arrived to the huge study where biscuits and wine awaited us. I had my glass and was about to refill it when Fortini himself entered, picked up a bell from his huge desk and rang the meeting to order. We all sat down, some twenty people, priests, monks and writers, in a semicircle, facing the Avvocato, who, standing under his own portrait, announced in response to so many of his guests' expressions of sorrow at his resignation as mayor that he was glad to be able from now on to devote himself exclusively to studying the life of St Francis and thus make his small contribution to the world at large rather than to the local affairs of his town. Then, as usual, he picked up his work in progress, sat down and began taking us further along on St. Francis's last journey to Egypt in 1219. As I listened, my eyes wandered over the shelves, filled with books and leather-bound volumes of documents, newspaper clippings and texts of Fortini's speeches; over the glass showcase displaying his medals; and occasionally, I must admit, they stopped at the carafe of excellent wine standing on his desk. I could not help feeling impatient, my mind wondering what Fortini wanted to talk to me about. Until a few weeks ago, nobody outside my own flock at San Damiano had discussed with me anything of consequence, but suddenly I had become the Bishop's man of trust, I was called upon to persuade nuns to hide Jews, and now the Mayor—or rather, the ex-Mayor—wanted to consult me on some important matter.

Fortini was one of the most colourful men Assisi had produced. His friends included the King himself, Victor Emmanuel III, who out of his esteem for the Avvocato had let him arrange the wedding of his daughter, Princess Giovanna, to King Boris of Bulgaria in our own Basilica of St Francis. He was an intimate of Gabriele d'Annunzio, one of our greatest writers and war heroes, and they say that whenever Fortini visited him at Villa Vittorale on Lake Garda, d'Annunzio would welcome him with a 21-gun salute—from his hunting rifle. And finally, Fortini was a close associate of Mussolini, at whose side he had marched on Rome and at whose side he had faithfully remained for over twenty years. But now his three powerful friends had vanished. D'Annunzio had been dead for five years and the two others no longer worked hand in hand. One was a German ally, the other an American and British ally, and each was raising five Italian divisions to fight the other. How did Arnaldo Fortini fit into this scheme of things? He did not, and so he chose the wisest possible course—he bowed out of politics altogether, letting Stadtkommissar Stolmann name a new mayor, Alcide Checconi, who, unlike Fortini, was more of a Fascist than a monarchist and therefore more cooperative with the Germans.

After the reading, there was the usual applause and compliments, chicory and more biscuits were served, the rest of the wine drunk, handshakes exchanged, and then finally the door closed behind the last guest. The Avvocato waved me to a chair near to him. 'Padre,' he said in a hushed tone of voice, 'I have a problem and I went with it to the Bishop. He told me I should speak to you and trust you in this matter.' He then told me, somewhat hesitantly, that the day before, one of his acquaintances, Professor Emilio Viterbi of the University of Padua, had come to his house. He was a very important scientist, a former collaborator of Enrico Fermi. He was also a Jew. He asked

Fortini to hide all his scientific papers, which the Avvocato did, and also to hide him and his family, which obviously he could not, considering the continuous traffic of people to the Villa Fortini. The Professor, his wife and two daughters were staying at the Hotel Sole on the Corso Mazzini, which, being in the city centre, was highly dangerous. What is more, they were waiting for some of their relatives and friends to join them. They expected, Fortini explained, that Assisi, because of its religious significance, would be declared an open city and as such barred to the German troops. Little did they know that the first razzia in town had already taken place.

From the uncertain way Fortini approached me, I felt sure that Nicolini had not told him about the other Jews already hiding here. I told my host that yes, I would take care of the new arrivals and I was glad that he didn't ask me where I would place them. I was already prepared for a further influx of Jewish refugees. The Sisters of St Colette had agreed to hide them in their cloister, and the German Sisters who used to run a guest-house for Germans were now ready to extend their hospitality to their victims. And of course there was always room in my own convent of San Damiano.

The Avvocato rang the bell. His daughter entered and he asked her to bring us more wine. Wine was now scarce and, when you could get it, it was watery. But Fortini's wine was not bad, not bad at all. He filled the glasses to the brim, we drank, and then I got up. But Fortini waved me back to my seat. He had something to show me, he said, and from a drawer he pulled out a sheet of typewritten paper. 'This is a copy of my letter to the Pope,' he said. 'I want you to have it. I sent it before my resignation and let's hope it will do us all some good. Read it,' he added, but before I could do so he pulled out his own copy and started to read it to me himself.

'In my capacity as the Mayor of Assisi and the President of the International Society for Franciscan Studies,' Fortini spoke as if presenting a case in court, 'I consider it my duty to ask your Holiness to give your urgent attention to the peril our city is exposed to in the current war. Assisi is the cradle of Franciscan faith. The tomb of the patron saint of our country and that of St Clare rest in the basilicas that are under the direct protection of the Vatican. Our numerous holy places associated with our Saints, our ancient churches and convents, the precious religious works of art by Cimabue, Giotto, Simone Martini and others belong to the entire world. The town is of no political significance—having a population of only five thousand. It has no industrial importance, as there are no factories within its walls. It has no military significance—there are no army barracks or military installations. Nor does it have any topographical importance, lying away from the main road and railway. On the other hand, the town is one of the great spiritual centres of the Christian world, visited by some 200,000 pilgrims annually, and it ranks, together with Rome and Jerusalem, as one of the sacred Christian cities. I therefore have the honour to ask your Holiness to appeal to the belligerent parties to agree not to introduce any troops or military supplies into our town and to proclaim it an open city, in order to spare it from wartime destruction. 3 October 1943. Avvocato Arnaldo Fortini, Mayor of Assisi, President of the International Society for Franciscan Studies.'

My host finished reading his letter and turned to me. 'What do you think of it?'

I was moved and I told him so. He wrote beautifully and I was sure that the Pontiff would be convinced by his arguments. The question, of course, remained, whether the Germans would be convinced as well. After refusing another glass of wine—after all, greed is a sin—I turned to go but the Avvocato, mellowed by the drink, offered to accompany me all the way to the gate of his villa. And as we walked along the cypress-lined avenue, he put his arm around my shoulders and said he wanted to confide something else in me. And that was that St Francis was Jewish, too. How otherwise could one explain his love for and continuous use of the Star of David? Or the fact that, after his death, Jews from all over the world contributed so much to the Franciscan Order? He, Fortini, was planning to do considerable research on the subject and then, of course, to write a book about it. But he had no doubt. St Francis was a Jew. Just like Christ.

As I walked down the narrow, winding streets, past old women dressed in black sitting in their doorways, sewing their linen, I pondered about Fortini's new theory concerning our patron saint. Somehow his idea sounded far-fetched to me. But I was glad, for it had probably helped Professor Viterbi and his family.

A week or so after my visit to the Villa Fortini, I sat at the Cafe Minerva, enjoying my Wednesday game of checkers with Luigi Brizi. It was a pleasant afternoon and the people of Assisi were in the Piazza Comune, exchanging the gossip of the day. The young signorine had already begun their traditional 'passegiata', parading in small groups, arms linked, between the Basilicas of St Francis and St Clare, enjoying the admiration of the few young men who had miraculously been left in town instead of being taken into the army. The signores of the city sat with their wives at the Cafe Excelsior, sipping chicory and eating fancy saccharine-sweetened maize cakes, while the shopkeepers, the artisans and we, the poor monks, were grouped on the other side of the piazza fountain, at the Minerva, around jugs of watered down red Umbrian wine. 'Fortini is waving to you,' Brizi said as he looked up from the board, waiting for me to make a move.

I turned and saw the Avvocato at the Excelsior getting up from his table and beckoning to me to come forward. I excused myself and got up quickly. Fortini met me more than half-way, by the lion fountain. 'I have received an answer from the Vatican,' he said, very excited. 'My letter had an effect. The Holy See has intervened.'

He then told me that, though the Germans had turned down the idea of declaring Assisi an open city, they had agreed to convert our town into a hospital and convalescent centre for their wounded soldiers, thus ensuring that the city would not be bombed and would therefore be spared the ravages of war. Still, it would take a few weeks before the Vatican could get word to the Allies and secure their approval. But the Holy See was optimistic about the outcome.

That was good news, indeed, and I congratulated Fortini on his splendid achievement. He returned to the Excelsior and I to the Minerva. As I waited for Brizi, who had still not made his move, my enthusiasm paled somewhat. A few weeks, especially during a war, was a long time. And the bombing of our city was not the only thing that I was worried about.

VI

I was worried not only about my charges, whose number grew daily, but whether Brizi, my opponent at checkers, would become my partner in the underground and print the Aryan papers that we needed. It was that very Wednesday afternoon that I had planned to talk to him. We had to try to get as many Jews as possible out of the country while the going was good. In Genoa, Cardinal Boetto had a means of getting them on board neutral ships and Cardinal della Costa of Florence had organised a whole network of parish priests who helped to smuggle them into Switzerland. But to embark on these journeys, the Jews had to have different names. As Kropfs or Baruchs they would never even reach Perugia.

And time was running short. The last few days had brought scores of Jewish refugees from Rome, who carried with them terrible tales of people being snatched from the streets and dragged from their homes. A thousand were transported on 18 October to Birkenau concentration camp. This was just three weeks after the Nazis had extorted from the Jews of Rome a tribute of fifty kilograms of gold with the promise of leaving them in peace. Other cities, I had no doubt, would suffer the same fate as Rome, and one could never be sure when the next razzia would take place in our own town, with the Germans perhaps breaking into the cloistered areas of the convents.

That afternoon Luigi not only won all his games, but was also treated by *me* to a glass of wine. As this had never, never happened before, he looked at me more attentively and somewhat uneasily, as if he suspected I was up to something. 'What did Fortini tell you?' he asked. I told him. He shrugged. 'Won't make much difference. Our own people will see to it that "alles ist in Ordnung", as the Germans say. We have the OVRA, the Fascist House and the Blackshirt Brigades to spy on us and to report to the Gestapo.' He drained his glass and got up, adjusting his black tie and black borsalino. 'Well, I've to go back to work. See you next Wednesday.'

'Let's take a walk, Luigi,' I said, digging out all the lire I had to pay the bill. 'I have some business to discuss,' I added quickly.

'Printing for the monastery?'

'For the monasteries,' I corrected him. It was the Bishop who had said that, having succeeded in swaying the nuns with my gift of the gab, as he put it, persuading an old man to help us would be child's play. I was not so sure. For the nuns, death was but a welcome step to paradise. Brizi believed only in life on earth—and this one life he wanted to live.

The ancient lanes were wrapped in a gentle autumn mist that rose slowly as we started to walk. Cooing flocks of doves strutted over the tiled roofs. From different parts of Assisi church bells began to toll for vespers. 'A beautiful town,' I said.

'Yes.'

'No other town matches ours. Not Perugia, not Siena, not Florence. And proud—Assisi has a proud history.'

Luigi glanced at me uneasily. 'You're not going to talk to me about St Francis?'

'Oh, no. I know you're not a religious man. But you see,' I clasped the old man's arm, 'it's by far more pleasing to God to know that a man is good at heart than to see him sit through mass without paying attention to it.'

Luigi scratched his ear. 'Business, Father. You said you had some business.'

We came to a small piazza and I halted on the corner in front of its name, as if I had never seen it before. 'Piazzetta Garibaldi,' I read, slowly and deliberately. 'The general without whom there would not be an Italy, only dozens of principalities and cities, many of them under foreign domination. He fought against the huge Austrian army, with 12,000 soldiers, and won, and on his expedition to Sicily against the Bourbons he took with him only one thousand, but he won again.' I resumed my walk and we entered a narrow, winding street. I stopped again. 'Via Eugenio Brizi,' I read, then turned to Luigi. 'Any relation?'

Brizi indignantly adjusted his tie and borsalino. 'You know damn well who he was, Padre. The city's Mayor, a colleague and friend of Garibaldi and Mazzini, a fighter for Italian unity and democracy—and my father's uncle.'

'Yes,' I said, 'I know that. Did you know other friends of Garibaldi and Mazzini? Did you know that in his army of 12,000 against Austria, Garibaldi had 400 Jews, and that among the thousand members of the Sicilian expedition, eight were Jews, including two high-ranking officers?' The history of the Italian Jews which Otto Maionica had lent me had served me well.

'No, I didn't know that,' Luigi muttered, not understanding what I was driving at.

'And that without the financing of Mondolfi of Florence', I continued, 'and Todros and Avigdor of Turin, Mazzini would not have succeeded, and without the Rothschilds' money, Cavour would not have succeeded either.'

Brizi stopped now. 'What the hell are you driving at, Padre?'

'There is the Via Portico,' I pointed ahead, 'and there is a plaque on the house where your great-uncle lived. He was a hero, he was a democrat, a liberal; he fought against the foreigners and for the independence of Italy, and he fought the privileged classes for the equal rights of all citizens—*together* with Mazzini, Cavour and Garibaldi. When I speak to you about the glory of Assisi, I am not speaking about St Francis, but about your uncle, Luigi. He is up there'—I pointed dramatically at the sky—'ashamed of you! Because you, here, are doing nothing for Italy, nothing for democracy!'

Luigi pulled out a handkerchief and wiped his face. His eyes blinked distractedly. 'What am I supposed to do? And, for heaven's sake, what have the Jews got to do with it?'

'In 1925, thirty Jewish intellectuals signed a manifesto against Mussolini; in 1938, twenty-five Jewish generals and five admirals were dismissed from the Italian Army when the racial laws were re-enacted. Jewish editors—and printers—who published *L'Indipendente* and *Il Piccolo* during the Risorgimento risked their lives for our country. The Finzi family gave Italy generals, writers and senators who supported Garibaldi—and there is a Finzi here, hiding in the Convent of the Stigmata, not knowing whether he will be caught tomorrow by the Nazis and Fascists. The Fanos of Milan were supporters of Mazzini and your uncle—and there is a Fano, hiding in the convent of St Colette. Luigi Brizi, are you going to help them?'

'Jews? Here, in Assisi?'

'Yes.'

'How?' Luigi cried. 'How can I help them?' The old man seemed close to tears.

'By printing false identity cards in your printing shop. By contributing to the cause you preach yourself—freedom and democracy. By repaying the debts Mazzini, Garibaldi, Cavour *and* Brizi owed them. By saving their lives.'

We came to the main street of the city. 'I know, I know!' Brizi expostulated, pointing to the sign with the name of the street. 'I can read!' And he walked on down the Corso Mazzini, shaking his head and deep in thought.

We reached the Via Santa Chiara, the road where Brizi's gift shop and printing press were. In the front room, filled with the Umbrian ceramics and metalwork that Brizi sold, was a stocky man with a square face, limping around as he walked. This was Luigi's son, Trento. I pointed to a taxi standing on the Piazza Santa Chiara. 'Your friend, Geremia del Bianco,' I said. 'He has been bringing in Jews trying to escape from Nazi deportation.'

The muscles in Brizi's withered face twitched. 'Geremia? Geremia has been doing it? He never told me.'

'Obviously not. Just as you'll keep to yourself what you are going to do for the Jews. Our convents are filled with those hapless people, and we, monks and nuns, are risking our lives for their sake.'

'How many identity cards do you need?' Luigi asked, swallowing hard, his voice quavering.

'About a hundred and fifty. Oh, I knew I could count on you!' And I grabbed the old man's hand. 'Your name, Luigi, will be as famous for your patriotic and liberal work in the twentieth century as your uncle's was in the nineteenth. And who knows, perhaps one day, there will be a Via Luigi Brizi running parallel with Eugenio Brizi's, and a plaque right here on this shop, saying...'

Luigi sighed. 'How do you propose to make those identity cards?'

'Easy. I already have samples from various southern communities. We copy their text and lettering and, of course, will fill in the names ourselves. Our Jews will become Catholic refugees from the south, with papers signed by officials now under Allied control and—unreachable.'

'You have missed your vocation, Padre,' Luigi said, and he smiled. 'You should have been a diplomat, not a monk.' Then he added, 'I will do it—on one condition. I don't want my son, Trento, to know, to be involved at all. In case something happens to me, I do not want him to be incriminated. I've only one son and he's already had his share of suffering, being wounded in the fighting in Croatia and being invalided out of the army.'

'That's a deal.' And once more I shook the man's hand, to seal our agreement that he was now a member of our 'underground'.

'The nights are best for work. I often stay in the shop, even during the curfew, when there is an urgent job. And no one in the street can hear the noise from the back room. When do you want to start?'

'Tonight.'

Luigi closed his eyes and sighed again. 'Tonight, then.' But after a moment's reflection he added that he needed someone to help him and to watch the street through the window, just in case. And as soon as a batch of documents was printed, the type would have to be distributed before his son or anyone else had a chance to discover any trace of the work.

'Good,' I said. 'I'll come a few minutes before the curfew—to start my new job as a printer's apprentice.'

When I returned to Luigi's shop that evening, the front door was closed and the windows shuttered. I looked around, saw no one and knocked. A moment later the door opened and Luigi's hand guided me across the dark room, through another door, to his printing shop. The light from a small bulb hanging from the ceiling revealed Brizi in his overalls and black beret. I took in the foot-operated press and the shelves filled with rows of metal letters. 'You have a nice set-up here.'

Luigi scoffed. 'They used that kind of machinery before the war—the First World War that is.' From under my habit I pulled an envelope containing samples of identity cards procured by the Bishop himself from the Catholic refugees from the south who were now in hiding in his palace. Luigi examined several of them. 'Good,' he said. 'They all use the same text and same lettering, probably from a government-prescribed form. The difficult part is the front page. Here, I imagine, the provincial authorities were allowed to exercise their individuality, and the designs of the national emblem—the Cross of Savoy—and the text and the printed characters vary with each city and province. Well, I have quite a collection of different emblems and I hope I'll be able to find the right ones. Anyway, let's get to work. Inside pages first, they are all the same.'

For several hours, I watched him work, trying to help whenever I could. Occasionally I would walk into the front room and look through the shutter slits at the empty piazza. It was around midnight when Luigi picked up a proof and looked at it with satisfaction, then passed it on to me. The left inner page bore the usual questions in italics: surname, name, father, mother, date and place of birth, marital status, nationality, occupation, residence, height, weight, hair, eyes, birthmarks. The right side provided a space for a photograph stamped by the seal of the commune, the signature of the bearer, the date of issue, the signature of the mayor and also space for the fingerprint of the left index finger.

'Very good,' I complimented the old man.

'Now for the front.' He picked up a sample. 'Catanzaro', he read. It was a town in the south, in Calabria. He started to look through his collection of emblems, but suddenly halted, raised his head and signalled to me to keep still. He switched the light off. We remained motionless, aware of the sound of boots, rhythmical and hollow on the pavement. I slipped out of the room and through a slit in the shutters I saw the shadows of two men blocking my view. Holding my breath, I listened to quiet voices, the click of a match, the polite exchange of the German 'Danke schön' and the Italian 'Prego', and then the shadows began to recede and two armed policemen, one German, one Italian, came into focus, smoking peacefully and strolling away from the shop. The dim, yellow light of a street lamp threw huge distorted silhouettes on to the piazza as the men crossed it and finally vanished into a side street. I returned to the back room, closed the door behind me and switched on the bulb. 'They've gone,' I said, giving Luigi a reassuring smile.

The old man went back to work, but after making a proof of the title page, he crumpled it up with disgust. 'The emblem is all right, but the type is all wrong.' With the Catanzaro identity card in his hand, he went to the shelves and began selecting new characters from their boxes, comparing them with those on the card, until finally he nodded approval. A few minutes later, he stepped on the pedal of the printing press and then smiled with relief. 'Perfect,' he said. 'Perfect! Now let's get the right paper.' Brizi picked up a sheet, felt it between his fingers, then reached for another from a different pile. He handed it to me; I repeated the touch test and nodded. 'Good,' Luigi said; 'let's get rolling!' He tightened the strings around the type of two inner pages, put it on the press, then fastened the screws around the plate. He stacked the paper in the machine's feedboard, filled its fountain with ink and pressed the pedal. 'Too much ink.' He adjusted the rollers and got a new proof out. 'Now, this is fine. How many?'

'Fifty is tonight's order for the Poor Clares, the Sisters of St Colette and San Damiano. Tomorrow you'll get a new batch of samples which Don Brunacci will obtain from *his* refugees. Unless you want to do all the inner pages tonight and hide them.'

'Oh, no, I won't take any risks. We'll break up the type but it will be easy to reassemble it again tomorrow.' He rubbed his hands and pushed the pedal. 'When they are dry, cut them on the trimmer. I'll show you how.' He removed the print composition from the machine. 'Now let's do the front page; a few from Catanzaro, and then we shall imitate other cities in the South—Bari, Naples, Foggia, Taranto.'

I offered Luigi a cigarette. The old man took one, lit it, and inhaled deeply. 'We still have a problem,' I said, 'with making the seals to be stamped over the photographs. The boys—the Jews hiding in San Quirico—have been working all day with some rubber I bought, but...' I made a grimace and pulled a sample of a Bari city stamp from my pocket.

'Amateur!' Luigi snorted. 'The authorities will detect it right away.'

'So what shall we do?'

'I'll make them, of course. What do you think a printer does—I mean a good printer! Just visiting cards, wedding invitations and announcements of deaths? Padre, I've made hundreds of rubber stamps.' He opened a drawer and picked out a black beret and a bottle, half filled with red country wine. 'You want to put this on?' I declined the beret, but I took the bottle from my host's hands. 'Take a good swig, Padre, we shall need it.' I raised the bottle to my lips and let the alcohol warm me, then passed the wine on to Luigi. After taking a long pull, Luigi threw the empty bottle into a wastepaper-basket and rolled up the sleeves of his shirt.

'I'm beginning to enjoy this,' he said. 'Both the printing and making fools out of the Fascists.'

VII

The city seals gave us our biggest headache. We had to have several, since our hundred and fifty refugees could not come from just two or three cities. And though Luigi knew his job well, making a convincing rubber stamp proved to be a very slow process.

Meanwhile I kept my friars busy. Some of them went to the Central Post Office to find names and addresses from the telephone directories of the southern provinces. Others bought stamps, a few at a time, in different tobacconists' shops, as these had to be fixed to the documents.

But finally, one late afternoon in November 1943, we opened our 'passport office' in the cloister of San Quirico for business. To celebrate the occasion, the moment I entered the convent, I pulled out from under my habit some presents for the sisters since they were running short of supplies. Suora Alfonsina, an extern in charge of shopping, was wise to the ways of the outside world. 'Black market?' she asked.

'No, compliments of the Lord Bishop.' The nun opened a side gate that led to the secluded garden. Since the razzia, I, as the Father Guardian of the Jews, was admitted to the cloister to take care of my flock. There, behind the oleanders, flower-beds and vegetable patches, stood an oblong one-storey building attached to the main one. It was here that the Jewish refugees lived.

An old table had been placed in one of the rooms and behind it sat the 'officials'. The identity cards had already been filled in by Giorgio Kropf on his battered portable typewriter, using fictitious Christian names. For a while I watched the proceedings. At one side of the table sat Nino Maionica, Otto's nephew. He took the photographs from discarded documents and trimmed away any previous stamp marks. Giorgio, sitting in the middle, would then take the corresponding identity card from the pile, glue the picture to it, find the appropriate city seal, ink it and press it once over the picture and once over the state stamps on the back page. Then Pali Jozsa, sitting on his left, would take the card from Giorgio and call out: 'Giovanni Pastore' or 'Lia Romeo', and ask that person to sign his or her assumed name. Finally, Carlo, Nino's brother, would take the person's index finger, rub it on the ink pad and press it in the space provided, and then, with his compliments, deliver the new identity card to its owner.

'Look, Padre,' Nino Maionica handed me his own identity card. 'Martorana,' I read. 'Enrico. Father: Carlo. Mother: di D'Amore Maria; born 31 December 1909 in Caserta. Bachelor. Italian. Residence: Via Luigi Vanvitelli 8, Caserta'... 'Beautiful!' I said.

I now had to go to Florence to prepare the escape route for my charges. With these documents, all would be well. But still our printing work would not be finished. A whole new group of refugees had arrived at San Damiano the previous evening and, following the example of Father Sebastian of Santa Maria degli Angeli, I had them all dress in monks' habits and was teaching them how to say the Kyrie Eleison. And an hour before my arrival at San Quirico I not only got salt and sugar from the Lord Bishop, but also a new order for false identity cards for Jewish refugees hiding in Perugia.

As I was about to leave, old Baruch pulled my sleeve. 'We have a problem, Padre,' he said. He started to walk with me towards the gate. 'With a primus the sisters gave us, we set up a kosher kitchen in the convent, for the few of us who are orthodox Jews.'

'What's kosher?' I asked. There was nothing about the Jewish religion in the book that Maionica had lent me. As a matter of fact, there had been an amusing incident a few weeks earlier. The sisters, having learned about another forthcoming Jewish holiday, had prepared a sumptuous meal for their charges. Then to their dismay they found it was Yom Kippur, the day of atonement and fasting. They had no choice but to consume it themselves, hoping that God and St Clare would forgive them their indulgence.

'Kosher', Baruch explained, 'means that one cannot mix milk and meat products and one must have two separate sets of pots and dishes. But as no meat is available nowadays, that is not the problem I want to talk to you about.'

'It wouldn't have been a problem even in pre-war times,' I said. 'The Poor Clares dispensed with meat long ago.'

'Still,' Baruch went on, 'the sisters ran out of oil, so they now use lard for cooking. Lard is a meat product. Could you get us some oil, please?'

I nodded. Another problem—oil was even more scarce than salt and sugar, and these three items had practically replaced money as a means of exchange.

Brizi was in the shop selling postcards to German pilots when I came in. Trento helped his father only in the mornings; in the afternoons he took long siestas, still recuperating from his leg wounds. I returned the airmen's greetings and busied myself with examining a ceramic relief of St Francis stroking a lamb. When the Germans left, Luigi said, 'You're earlier today, aren't you? Restless because it's our last night, eh?'

I glanced at the door, to make sure that no one was coming in, then sighed. ''Not the last, I'm afraid. There are more documents to prepare. The Bishop got word that a number of Jewish refugees are hiding in the San Andrea Church in Perugia.'

'And now they are all coming to Assisi?'

'No, but they all need identity cards. Apparently the priests and monks there have also been hiding Jews.'

Luigi shook his head and blinked nervously. 'Don't they have a printer there who could do the job as well as I could?'

'No, Luigi,' I insisted; 'you're unique, and history will record that.'

The old man swallowed hard. 'How many?' he asked, after a moment of inner struggle.

'Seventy. And soon they will all be leaving for Genoa and escaping from Italy—thanks to you. The Bishop has asked me to convey his blessings for you and your family.'

Little Luigi straightened up. 'Tell the Bishop', he said, 'that I'm not doing it for the Church. I'm doing it for Italy.'

I heard footsteps and turned round. Trento stood in the shop's threshold. 'Still working tonight, Father?'

'Yes,' Luigi said. 'I've a few more nights of urgent work.'

'Good, I'll stay to help you.' Without a word, Trento limped into the back room and returned in black, printing overalls, long discarded by his father. 'Do you think, do you *both* think that I'm a fool? That I couldn't guess what you two were doing at night? Be glad it's me and not the OVRA people who found a proof jammed in the machine. Since when are you the official printer of the City of Palermo? Father, whatever you are doing, I've completely recovered now and am ready to help you.'

Luigi looked at me awkwardly as if seeking advice. Then his eyes travelled back to his son. 'I didn't want you to be involved, Trento, you understand?'

'I want to be involved,' Trento answered. 'I want to be with you all the way.' Once more he went into the printing room and returned with two berets. He handed one to his father and put on the other himself. 'I'm ready to start!'

Luigi's face broke into a slow smile. He approached his son and slapped his back with all the strength and all the affection he had. 'God,' he said, 'you are a Brizi!' Then he turned to me. 'Give me the new list.' I handed it to him.

'Good,' I said. 'I've skipped a lot of my canonical hours. I hope God will forgive me.'

Trento rubbed his hands in anticipation. 'Brizi & Brizi are now in business,' He winked at me.

'Don't be impatient,' his father said. 'We must wait until curfew. Go, Padre, and make up for your missed prayers. You know the Brizis aren't church-goers, but one mustn't take chances, so include us in them. We can use all the help we can get.'

'I will. I may have missed prayers, but I've learned a trade.'

The old man broke into a loud guffaw. 'Padre, do you know what we call someone who does the job you have been doing? I didn't want to tell you in case you might be offended. The printer's devil. Because the printer's apprentice is always smeared with ink and looks like an assistant to Mephisto himself.'

'Goodbye, Mephisto,' I laughed. 'You're doing a hell of a job and God bless you for it.'

Outside on the pavement I halted and gratefully breathed in the cold autumn air. I had spent two whole weeks in that shop, night after night. How many trials and ordeals, how many disappointments and satisfactions at a job well done, how many bottles of wine and packets of cigarettes! And how many times our hearts had stopped at the sound of soldiers' footsteps loud in the silent curfew nights!

Then I started to walk fast back to my monastery, where I knew I would still have to spend an hour or so before vespers, teaching paters and aves to the new class of postulants who, only a few days ago, had come to San Damiano from the ghettoes of northern Italy.

VIII

The moment I left the station, I sensed that something unusual was going on in the town. Truckloads of armed German soldiers were rushing through the streets, and helmeted Gestapo men, with guns slung across their chests, roared past on motorcycles. Time and again I came across a roadblock manned by the Italian Fascist police, checking private vehicles or the few passers-by who ventured into the streets. As I approached the city centre, I heard loudspeakers and finally could make out the words: 'Achtung! Attenzione! All inhabitants outside! No packing, take nothing. You have three minutes.'

I was in Florence to see Cardinal Della Costa, to arrange for the transport of our first group of refugees to Genoa or Switzerland. Personally I had nothing to fear. I was a monk, with a proper identity card, and a letter to explain my mission—to secure food from the Cardinal's stores for Catholic refugees in Assisi. The Cardinal was our Archbishop, too, Bishop Nicolini's superior.

A few minutes later I reached the Via Pucci, where a black Mercedes was standing next to an empty truck, with an officer holding a megaphone to his mouth. Then I saw storm-troopers in black uniforms, with twin silver flashes on their collars and death's heads on their black helmets, coming out of the building, pushing people with their rifle butts; and—to my horror—I saw not only a group of men and women whom I guessed to be Jewish, but also a priest. I waited no longer.

All the streets leading towards the Archbishop's Palace presented the same picture—a truckload of SS troops, soldiers leading men and women out of their houses at gunpoint, officers shouting through megaphones or, incredibly, taking photographs to send home. I saw babies being snatched from their mothers' arms, as the Nazis split up parents and children, driving the children away in separate vehicles. I saw young men trying to run for their lives and being shot down. I saw a whole family lined up against a wall and machine-gunned, because a revolver had been found on one of them. When I reached the Piazza San Giovanni and entered the gate of the Archbishop's Palace, I was drenched in sweat. I had seen a razzia in Assisi before but never had I witnessed killing and executions in the street. That day was a memorable one in the history of Florentine Jews—23 November 1943. One thousand Jews were arrested and deported.

The Cardinal's secretary, Monsignore Giacomo Meneghello, came down to meet me. I knew him from my previous visit. As he walked towards me, he threw up his hands in the typical Italian gesture of despair. 'What a time to come!' he said. 'You're aware of what's going on here?' I told him what I had seen on my way, including the arrest of the priest. The Monsignore's face turned paper-white. 'Oh, God, I hope not! Via Pucci did you say? God, God!' he kept repeating. 'The fifth floor of No. 2 Via Pucci was the meeting-place of the five-man committee in charge of Jews in hiding. Was one of the men young, handsome, tall, with a black beard?' I nodded. 'The Chief Rabbi of Florence,' he said. 'Reverend Nathan Cassuto. And the priest was certainly Don Leto Casini.' It took him a while to compose himself. 'I have a room for you. You have probably travelled all night and will want to rest.'

To rest? At a time like this? I wanted to see the Cardinal and then go back. I was worried about my town, my own people; perhaps there was a razzia there too. But the Cardinal was not in, the Monsignore said. He had been out since morning, since, as Maneghello put it, 'la caccia del Ebreo', the Jew-hunt, had begun. I might as well go to my room; there was a Bible there I could read, and today's newspaper. And he would send me some food.

He pulled a bell cord and a servant led me to a small, austere room. There was a bed in it, but I did not lie down. I knelt before a crucifix and prayed—I prayed with all my heart—for the hunted Jews of Florence, for the Chief Rabbi and his companion the priest, for the mothers who had lost their children, and for their children who until now had known only love and were too small to comprehend the meaning of human hate. I prayed for the souls of those who were shot on the street and left there like stray animals. I paid no attention as the servant tiptoed into the room, to leave a plate of food on the table. I then swore to God and my patron saint, that, as long as I lived, I would do all I could to help those living and hiding to live and hide in peace. When I got up, I ate and drank a cup of chicory, not because I was hungry or thirsty but because I knew I must try to keep up my strength; then I lay down. But I could not sleep. I picked up the paper, not the Bible; I did not need it now, I had just spoken with God. But as my eyes fell on the front page of *Il Popolo d'Italia* my stomach knotted in alarm. There, a black-bordered two-column announcement screamed an 'Order of the Ministry of the Interior, Social Italian Republic, No. 5: All Jews residing in Italy, irrespective of their nationality, are to present themselves on 30 November at the concentration camps listed below. All their goods, moveable and immoveable, are subject to immediate requisition and will be given to people who have suffered as the result of enemy bombardment and war damage.'

I must have fallen asleep after all, from sheer exhaustion. When I woke up, I saw Meneghello standing over me. 'The Cardinal is back,' he said. Then, while I was washing my face, he told me that the Chief Rabbi and Don Leto had been caught. A hundred people had been taken away. The worst raid had happened at the Carmine Convent where the Dominican nuns were taking care of Jewish orphans. The Nazis had snatched fifty of them; only two little girls were saved. Suora Luisa, the Mother Superior, had managed to hide them under her habit.[1]
'Come, Father, His Eminence is waiting for you.'

Elia, Cardinal della Costa, Archbishop of Florence, sat in a swivel chair, his face buried in his hands, resting on his buhl desk. There was a splendour here that was absent from Bishop Nicolini's reception room. The walls were adorned with the gilded portraits of former archbishops of Florence and the mahogany shelves filled with leather-bound volumes. The floor was covered with Aubusson carpets and the windows were framed by brocade curtains. His Eminence looked up and I saw that his face was drawn, with tired lines around the eyes. 'We have been expecting you, Padre,' he said. 'Please sit down.'

I knelt and kissed the Cardinal's ring, then sat on a chair at the other side of the desk. 'I'm sorry', I said, 'that I came on a day like this, to add to the troubles Your Eminence already has on his hands.'

'Go on, Padre. The razzia is over—at least for today,' he said. I saw him making an effort to give me his undivided attention.

'I came here in the hope that Your Eminence could give me the kind of assistance he granted me last time. We have quite a number of Jews hiding in our area whom we would like to

---

[2]All fifty perished in concentration camps; of the two survivors, Elena Silberstein died a year later of beri-beri: her sister, De Susanna Ceccherini, lives in Rome.

move, in small groups of course, to Genoa or to the Swiss border to get them out of the country. We have provided them with the proper documents.'

'I know,' the Cardinal answered. 'I've seen them. They are so good that no one would doubt their authenticity.' I was amazed. How could he have seen them? He explained that a few days earlier a group of Jews had come from Perugia, with the same request as mine. Their papers had been checked frequently en route to Florence, and they told the Cardinal where they had got them. 'How did you do it?' della Costa asked, his large green eyes for the first time twinkling with admiration.

'We have a clever printer,' I answered, then, encouraged by his smile, I asked, 'When can we send our first group?'

Cardinal della Costa fell silent; he frowned and I could see the pain he was feeling. 'You have come too late, I am afraid. The Perugia people are stranded here. They were at the Monastery of San Marco and their papers were checked and they were left alone. We no longer have an escape route. The port of Genoa has been infiltrated by the Gestapo, by the OVRA and by dock workers who work for the Gestapo and OVRA. Even the six hundred Jewish children for whom Pietro Boetto had already obtained visas to Turkey were unable to leave the country.'

'And Switzerland?'

'I'm afraid it's the same there, at least for most of the Jews. The Swiss are now letting in only babies, pregnant women and old people. They turn the others back.'

My jaw dropped. 'What are we going to do?' I asked lamely. 'All this work, for nothing!'

The Archbishop straightened himself in his chair. 'What do you mean, for nothing? With such documents, with such marvellous documents, you have ensured the safety of your people. This is much, much more than thousands of their compatriots have. Forty thousand Jews are hiding all over Italy, in monasteries and churches and private homes—and how few, how very few of them can dare to leave their hiding-places.'

'We had such hopes,' I sighed. 'Such high hopes.'

'I have been very anxious to see you, Padre,' Cardinal della Costa said. 'Especially since this morning.' For a moment he toyed with the golden chain of his pectoral cross before continuing. 'You came here to ask my help in establishing a route out of Assisi. I would like to reverse the process—and establish a route *to* Assisi.'

'Your Eminence doesn't mean to suggest that all Jewish refugees come to Assisi?'

'Calm down, Padre. No, I don't mean to turn your city into the hiding centre for Jews. But I would like to turn it into the counterfeiting centre—where you could produce identity cards for the people who need them. First of all for those who are hiding in private houses and are in constant danger. Those people need your help, Padre. You have done a lot, I know, but you could do so much more.'

Nervously I laced and unlaced the cord of my cincture. 'I'm not a saint, Your Eminence. I'm a Franciscan, not St Francis. No matter what our patron saint did, God said to him that it wasn't enough. He had to do more and more to be able to reach Him. Am I on trial?'

'We all are,' the Cardinal said. 'The whole Church. God has chosen to use these terrible times to test His own Church. Are we going to fail Him? The Lord knows of no distinction between people,' Cardinal della Costa went on, relentlessly. 'Every human life is dear to Him. We must obey God rather than Man.'

Slowly I raised my face. I was no longer afraid. I made my obeisance and, as he helped me back to my feet, the Prince of the Church rewarded me with a smile of gratitude. He arose, and pulled the bell cord. Archbishop della Costa was seventy, tall and straight as a ramrod, his balding head covered by the red zucchetto. An attendant appeared at the door. 'Bring us some coffee, please. No chicory, coffee.'

The one thing I get out of this, I thought, is real wine at Bishop Nicolini's, and now real coffee at Archbishop della Costa's. Then I told the Archbishop that we were running very short of food. Even with the supplies sent by the Holy See for refugees, the rations—150 grams of bread a day, 800 grams of pasta and half a litre of oil per month—did not go very far.

'They say', della Costa answered my request with a little smile, 'that there are three things that God doesn't know—

what a Jesuit thinks, how many nuns there are in Rome, and where the Franciscans get all their money? Don't you have plenty stacked away in your Assisi coffers to be able to obtain all you need?' He saw that my face was impassive and not amused and he added quickly, 'We shall help you, Padre, with whatever we can.'

The attendant brought a tray with two cups of steaming black coffee. After I had finished mine, I asked a question that had been bothering me for a long time. 'Perhaps Your Eminence can explain to me why the Pope doesn't make a statement condemning the Nazi persecution of Jews? I remember reading that before his death Pope Pius XI commissioned an American Jesuit—wasn't his name John La Farge?—to write an encyclical attacking anti-Semitism. But Pius XI died before he had a chance to publish it. Why doesn't Pius XII announce, urbi et orbi, the text of that encyclical?'

The Cardinal smiled indulgently. 'You ought to understand that the Vatican is a state and the Pope is also a politician, a head of state. I've been in Rome long enough to understand the Pope's position. Instead of making meaningless declarations that would only antagonise the Germans, perhaps even make them occupy the Vatican itself, he issued orders—to save Jewish lives.'

'And Your Eminence received such an order?'

Cardinal della Costa twisted his seal ring around his finger. 'The Pontiff could not issue an express order. But we received his message loud and clear. How would Pietro Boetto in Genoa, Nicolini in Assisi, I here, and so many other archbishops and bishops all over Italy, provide a sanctuary for the Jews, if we did not feel that that is what His Holiness would wish us to do? Do you think the Pontiff does not know what we are doing? Or that in his own diocese—don't forget the Pope is also Bishop of Rome—over a hundred convents and over fifty churches and theological seminaries are hiding four thousand Jews, half of the Jews of Rome?'

'I understand', I said, not really understanding at all. Why the Pontiff could not issue an express order? Wasn't he the most powerful man, St Peter's representative on earth? To cover my confusion, I turned to practical matters. 'How do you propose,

Your Eminence, to forward the photographs to us and pick up the identity cards when they are ready?'

'I have my couriers. The photographs will reach you in a week. There is one more thing, Padre. The port of Genoa and the Swiss border are practically sealed off now, but there is one other route we must try. To smuggle people across the army front line to the south. I have some volunteers ready to do just that. And Assisi is so much closer to the front than Florence.'

'We shall be awaiting your orders, Your Eminence. And in case things get too hot in the north, please remember—we have six monasteries sheltering our Jews, but there are twenty more in and around the town ready to do the same.'

I went down on one knee and kissed the Cardinal's ring. 'I have some good news for you,' he said. 'By the time you return, your first Stadtkommissar will be leaving. A new one has been appointed, thanks to the intervention of the Holy See. A Catholic. It will make your life very much easier. Go with God, my son.'

A Catholic, I thought as I walked across the room to the door. Was not every third German soldier a Catholic?

IX

Lieutenant-Colonel Valentin Müller. That was the name that in mid-December went up on the door of the Stadtkommissar's office at the Hotel Subasio. He was certainly a Catholic, for the day after his arrival he went to mass at the Basilica of St Francis. What is more, he was a doctor, lending credit to the belief that our city would indeed become a hospital and convalescent centre for the wounded soldiers of the Third Reich.

All this news reached me at San Damiano, where I had been kept very busy by the continuous stream of Jewish refugees, forced from their cities by the Nazi razzias and by the Fascist order to present themselves at the concentration camp nearest to their place of residence. They came mostly at night, whole families, walking down from the mountains, carrying letters signed by priests, attesting that they had lost their homes in an Allied bombardment, or that they were making a pilgrimage to Assisi, and that they were good Catholics needing my assistance. I could see the hand of Elia della Costa in it. The Cardinal had said he would send me photographs of the people, but now he was sending me the people as well. For him it was easy—all he had to do was to pass the word around his diocese and that was that. But for me, for us at San Damiano, every knock at the gate could mean the OVRA or the Gestapo and execution by firing-squad. Whenever I heard a knock, I used to cross myself, and in the first half of December I must have crossed myself a hundred times. But as I lay on my bed, fully clothed, awake and apprehensive, it was reassuring to know that there were other Italians, not even monks or priests, who did not sleep either. Two kilometres away, Luigi and his son worked night after night on the documents that would bring a new life not only to the Jews of Florence whose photographs della Costa had sent me, but also to the frightened people at San Damiano waiting to be sent to one of our monasteries or to be moved on once more, this time under an assumed name, to lose themselves in the big cities.

But finally I had to risk going into the town to ascertain whether we were indeed safer under the new commandant—and whether I could perhaps relax long enough to sleep for twenty-four hours. Sleep! There was nothing I craved for more. But if I had worked myself up to this state of sheer exhaustion, I could only blame it on my own mistrustful nature. I was always afraid to delegate my duties to one of my monks. So it was I who had to open the gate of San Damiano, I who had to check whether the people sent to me were genuine refugees, and I who had to decide where to send them next.

I have to admit that it was with relief that I left the monastery. The countryside had always had a soothing effect on me, even though a cold northerly wind was already blowing. But the wind brought with it the scents of myrtle and rosemary and the languid cries of quail and the quiet tinkling of ox-bells, which to my ears was music no less religious than that of a

Gregorian chant. As I walked through the almost biblical setting, among the rocks and gnarled olive trees and bare vines growing on the dry terraces, I consoled myself that even though winter was coming, spring too would come again—for the land, for us, for Italy.

The view of Assisi perched on Monte Subasio made me stop for a moment. It never failed to stir me, this view—especially at sunset, when the departing golden rays imbued the tiled roofs of the ancient stone houses with a mysterious reddish hue. Ever since I had climbed up the steep road to my elementary school in Deruta, shoes in hand to save the leather, I had dreamed of mounting the winding lanes of Assisi, which I imagined must look so much like those of Jerusalem. Assisi was no longer my adopted city, it had become *my* city, *my* Jerusalem—to which I had finally ascended. Here I knew every man, woman and child, now all dressed in their Sunday best, greeting me on their way to vespers. And just as I knew the people of Assisi, I knew all its houses with their geranium-laden balconies, holy reliefs and wrought-iron lamps, and the pairs of doors, one for the living and one, now walled up, for the dead, through which in the middle ages the dead had been carried out, to prevent contamination.

I no longer felt tired as I reached the piazza and settled down at the still empty Café Minerva with my usual glass of wine, raising it to the few men around me in a wordless, festive salute. As I was looking for someone reliable to question, I saw the towering figure of Giovanni Cardelli approaching me with a board and chess set. 'A game, Padre?' he asked. I rarely played chess; checkers was my game, but though I did not relish the idea of losing to Cardelli he was definitely a man who would be able to supply me with all the information I needed. He was an intelligent man, a university graduate and an ex-cavalry officer, though unemployed at the moment, hence his presence at the café in the daytime. I nodded my agreement and he quickly snapped his fingers and called Renzi, the emaciated, consumptive waiter, to bring us two glasses of wine. 'For later,' he said when I protested. I looked at him the way Luigi had looked at me when I offered him wine. Cardelli no doubt wanted something from me, too, something more important than I wanted from him. Slowly he set up the chessmen on the board and made the first move. 'What do you want?' I asked. I never liked to beat about the bush.

He waited for the boy to put down the glasses, glanced over his shoulder and whispered, 'Shelter—for two officers who have deserted the army. Two anti-Fascists.'

'And who sent you to me?' I asked, suddenly angry with Bishop Nicolini, with Cardinal della Costa and his network of priests. I already had my hands full searching for sanctuary for the Jews and I was beginning to run out of places to hide them in, and now they wanted me to help with the Italian underground and with the thousands of army deserters roaming the Apennine mountains. Enough was enough—there were other cities and other monasteries and other monks in Italy.

'Your turn, Padre Rufino,' Giovanni said calmly. I made a move—the usual opening pawn gambit. For a while he pondered on a way to develop his attack, then pushed his queen across the board and said softly, too softly for a cavalry officer who had defended Rome in the hopeless fight against the Germans on 8 September, 'We are in the same boat, Padre. And we can help each other. Our and your underground must join forces.'

'I—I don't know what you are talking about.'

He smiled and smoothed his moustache. 'It's all right, Padre. We have our men in the Casa del Comune and the carabinieri and they can help you with intelligence work, so that you could be forewarned about an imminent razzia'—slyly, he leaned forward—'and alert your people at San Quirico. A monastery is indeed the safest place. One of our two men is a very important officer—Colonel Gay, a member of the General Staff of the Italian Army.'

San Quirico? That's all he knew, I thought. Nothing about twenty other monasteries. Some underground, some intelligence! We., perhaps they were just starting. I must be generous. And even if they were socialists, or, God forbid, communists, in time they could become very useful to us. 'Where are they?' I asked.

'In my house.'

Was I not right? 'Are you crazy? A hundred yards from the OVRA headquarters? Or do you have your men there, too?'

I was aware of the sarcasm in my voice and it put him on the defensive.

'They only arrived this morning.'

These men had to be removed from his house! If they were found, the Gestapo and OVRA might start another razzia. 'I'll take those two,' I said. 'But no more, understand? And for that you will keep me posted.' I raised the glass—his glass, because I had already drunk mine—and we clinched our deal. 'Send them to San Quirico tonight, before the curfew.' San Quirico was our headquarters and I was already thinking how eminently suitable a member of the General Staff would be as *our* own chief of staff. 'Now, Cardelli, tell me, what kind of a person is our new Commandante della Piazza?'

Cardelli looked over my shoulder, holding a chess piece in his palm. 'Why don't you ask him yourself?'

I turned and saw the tall, bespectacled German officer in his early fifties, accompanied by Alcide Checconi, strolling across the piazza, apparently being shown round the city for the first time by the corpulent new Fascist Mayor. Not only I, but everybody in the piazza, fell silent, watching the pair approach. Marshal Vivo, the head of the Carabinieri, splendidly dressed and bemedalled for a Sunday, arose from his table at the Excelsior and saluted smartly. The Mayor suggested that they should go over to him, but Müller shook his head. A moment later the two men stopped as Pietro Cogolli, the town's pharmacist and city councillor, rushed forward and introduced himself, pointing at his pharmacy and dramatically throwing his hands up, which could only mean that the town was running out of medical supplies and that he hoped the new commandant, who was a doctor, would see to it that his stocks would be replenished. Then the Colonel, with the Mayor a respectful step behind him, started towards our café. 'He is not only a colonel, he is also a politician,' Cardelli whispered. 'He does not need acceptance by the Fascists, he has it. He wants *our* approval. He will wait a long time!'

As the German selected a table close to ours, Checconi behind his back was frantically waving for us to get up. He breathed more easily when we finally lifted our posteriors from the chairs to pay our reluctant respects. He snapped his fingers at the waiter and ordered wine. The boy spread his hands, the bar owner came quickly, bowed his bald head and he, too, spread his hands. 'All right,' we heard Checconi sigh again. 'Vino di casa.'

A carafe and two glasses arrived in a second. As soon as the German officer's glass was filled, he took it, and apparently drawn to us by our game, approached our table and looked at our positions on the board. Again we arose and he waved us back to our seats. Cardelli made a move and then, while I was deciding what to do, my mind not at all on the game, the Colonel smiled at me, took a sip, then his smile turned sour like the wine he had drunk. He continued to hold the glass without touching the wine. I finally made a move, but his disapproving murmur arrested my hand in mid-air. Checconi decided to join us and introduce us to the Colonel. The German told us his name, and as if we did not know, explained that he was the nuovo Commandante della Piazza. 'You speak excellent Italian,' I said, disregarding the disapproving look in the eyes of my chess partner. Well, Cardelli had his ways, I had mine.

'Thank you,' he answered. 'I must pay you a visit, Padre. I want to see the place where St Francis and Brother Leone built the church to God.' I wished that damn Checconi had not mentioned San Damiano during his introduction.

'When?' I asked, swallowing hard. 'I would like to be prepared for your visit.'

'No need. I'll just drop by some time during the week.' He looked at Checconi. 'Shall we continue? I would like to pay my respects to your bishop.'

The bar owner refused to accept payment and that was all right with the Mayor, but not with the German officer, who insisted on paying and put five marks on the table, enough to treat the whole café to a drink. He saluted, we all got up again, and then the German and the Italian heads of the city walked away and disappeared under the great arch of the Palazzo dei Priori, which led past the house where St Francis was born to the palazzo where our bishop lived.

All over the town the bells sounded the end of vespers and people began descending the long steps from the Cathedral of San Rufino or climbing the narrow winding alleys from Santa

Maria Maggiore and St Peter's Abbey. They were all going to the piazza to walk and greet each other or to sit in the cafés and reminisce about the good old days before the war when coffee was coffee and wine was strong and undiluted. But the crowd was still quiet, ready to take part in another traditional ritual of the city, the farewell to the departing day—il crepuscolo, when sunset gives way to dusk, shadows lengthen, people begin to talk in hushed tones, the girls suddenly become more conscious of their youth and beauty and the boys more conscious of the girls. Even the doves on the roofs and the balconies begin to coo more gently. The distant rumble of trucks on the main highway gives way to the soft chorus of cicadas in the adjacent groves and the muffled cries of shepherds calling their sheep home. At such a time, especially on Sundays, you feel that the town has not changed since the middle ages and that from one of its side streets Brother Francis could at any moment emerge, in his sandals and rough tunic, accompanied by his flock of faithful disciples. I did not feel guilty about skipping my canonical hour, for I knew in my heart that my wordless communion with the holy town was no less important than the prescribed prayers. And, on this particular Sunday, when I'd played chess and drunk wine and the new German commandant had been exchanging pleasantries with us, my beloved city looked especially beautiful and peaceful—almost as if winter was already over and spring had just arrived.

There was no sleep for me that night either. Plans had to be made to disperse all the Jews among the neighbouring monasteries and we took them there, whether they already had new identity cards or not, handing men picks and hoes to carry, driving women and children away in ox-carts adorned with holy pictures. But the Colonel did not come that day or on the day after. On Wednesday, shortly after daybreak, I heard a knock at the gate, followed by the sound of a bicycle bell. I knew there was nothing to worry about, not only because there were no refugees at the convent but also because I knew whose bicycle it was. It belonged to Gino Battaglia, the former cycling champion of Italy, who at the age of thirty-two was already nicknamed 'Il Vecchio', 'the Old Man', because he had lost his title to the 22-year-old Fausto Coppi.

I got up, found my sandals in the dark, and rushed to the gate. There, in the wan light descending from the mountains, I saw the familiar tall, skinny figure, dressed in shorts and an undershirt, a peaked cap perched on his head. 'You'll catch cold, Battaglia!' I exclaimed.

He smiled. 'Thirteen kilometres from Perugia in a quarter of an hour is not bad, is it?' he said. He wheeled his bicycle into the courtyard.

Battaglia had already been twice to San Damiano, bringing photographs and then returning with identity cards a day or two later. He had always travelled in daytime, because his face was so familiar to the OVRA men and the police at the German checkpoints that they simply waved him on, convinced he was training. This time, he explained, he had spent the night at the Church of San Andrea in Perugia, since he had another day's ride to Abruzzi. On his return trip he would pick up the identity cards. As usual, he pulled the grips off his handlebars and unscrewed his seat, to take out the photographs and papers hidden inside the bicycle frame. I saw Fra Euralio getting ready for lauds and gave him the photos to hide in the Oratory of St Clare, among the holy relics in the cupboard.

'Come and have some coffee,' I said to Battaglia. Our coffee was made from barley, but my guest did not mind, and as we drank it in our refectory, he told me the purpose of his long journey. The Cardinal had asked him to contact a priest in Pescocostanzo called Don Paolo, also known as 'the smugglers' priest, because he had served as father confessor to those engaged in smuggling merchandise from the Allied-occupied territory across the Sangro river. The idea was, of course, to take people to the other side and make their trips profitable both ways. 'Good luck,' I said, relieved that, for a change, I had nothing to do with the new scheme.

I accompanied my visitor to the gate. Cockily, he slammed the cap on to his head. 'I got to Perugia in three hours forty-eight minutes,' he boasted. 'Ten minutes better than the last time. I'll be champion again one day. I'll show them who Il Vecchio is.' He pedalled away vigorously, waving goodbye to me before turning from the alley off into the track leading to the highway. He was a good cyclist and a good Catholic, Gino

Battaglia, and I feel sure these wartime assignments of his helped him to get into proper condition to win his title back from Coppi after the war.

An hour later, after lauds, I was on my way to San Quirico to check up on how the two Christian officers had been enlisted to work for my Jewish underground. I only hoped, as I was leaving, that Colonel Müller would not decide to visit us that early in the morning.

He came that afternoon. When I heard the heavy motor roaring down the rocky path from the direction of the city, I knew, we all knew, that the Stadtkommissar was on his way.

I rushed outside into the courtyard and waited at the end of the long poplar-shaded road. The open command car came to a halt. Colonel Müller greeted me with a military salute and then told his driver to wait. He alighted from the car and shook my hand. 'I have kept my promise, haven't I?' he said. Then his eyes travelled over the convent walls, to the little romanesque church in front of him. 'So it was here,' he said, reverently. He removed his hat and went inside, slowing his steps as he passed the wooden pews and approaching the bare wooden crucifix on the altar. He stared at it for a while, half closing his eyes, lit a taper, then knelt and buried his head in his hands, completely oblivious of my presence. I saw his lips moving, uttering Latin words. For a long time he remained motionless. Only after a quarter of an hour or so did he raise his head. I have seen this happen often, and yet I had to marvel that the German face did not look different from all the other Catholic faces refreshed after prayer. 'Will you show me around, Padre?' Müller said, and only now, when he rose to his feet and turned to follow me, did he notice the throng of friars peering at him curiously from the back of the church.

I took him into the cloister, which now housed men but which in the twelfth century had been assigned by St Francis to St Clare and her companions. We visited first the ancient refectory with its low ceiling and rough worm-eaten tables at which the Poor Clares had eaten their meagre rations of bread and water. In the nuns' dormitory I showed my visitor the brick floor on which St Clare slept, with a block of wood serving as her pillow. And then, in the oratory, I took out of the cupboard the flask containing St Francis's blood and the alabaster monstrance with which St Clare had chased the Saracens away, well aware that, hidden amongst the pages of an 800-year-old breviary, written by Fra Leone especially for St Clare, were the photographs brought earlier by Battaglia. Throughout this tour, Colonel Müller remained silent, listening attentively to my explanations. We finally walked into St Clare's little garden, where the nuns had built a hut of reeds for the half-blind St Francis, already bearing the wounds of the stigmata, some two years before his death. 'Wasn't it here', the Colonel asked, 'that St Francis wrote his Canticle of the Creatures?'

'Yes, on this stone behind you.' Müller turned and a warm smile broke out on his face when he discovered the text of the canticle inscribed on the stone. 'Most high omnipotent good Lord,' he read, 'Thine are the praises, the honour and all benediction. To Thee alone, most High, do they belong, and no man is worthy to mention Thee. Praised be Thou, my Lord, with all Thy creatures, especially the honoured Brother Sun...'

He was visibly moved. For a moment he looked at the countryside stretching before us, with its terraced vines and olive groves, then he raised his face to Monte Subasio. 'Eremo delle Carceri, the Hermitage is over there, isn't it?' I nodded. 'I have been in charge of the front-line hospital. At Monte Cassino. Being moved over to Assisi is like crossing from hell to heaven.' He shuddered.

'Can you drive me there?' he asked. I could hardly refuse, although the idea of the villagers seeing me in the German command car did not exactly appeal to me. I sat behind the Colonel and off we went, away from my brothers, who gaped at us open-mouthed, probably wondering whether I was being taken to the city for questioning.

'Is Assisi going to be a hospital and convalescent centre?' I asked as the car began to climb a steep road running through a forest of huge oaks.

'Yes, we are already preparing the city hospital, turning schools and hotels into sanatoriums.' This was both good and bad news. Good because we would be spared bombardments, bad because there would be so many more Germans in town—

wounded and convalescing soldiers, admittedly, but still enemy soldiers occupying our city and making my task more difficult.

We were gaining height continuously and suddenly the imposing mountain monastery came into view. A few of our charges were there, but I did not worry. They were all dressed in monks' habits and could recite the Kyrie and the Miserere and kneel for the Angelus at a moment's notice.

'How is it that you know so much about our Order?' I asked.

'I read up about it the moment I learned about my new posting. We are a very religious family.' From a wallet he pulled out a photograph of himself in army uniform, a broad middle-aged woman next to him and two blond teenagers, a boy and a girl. 'Taken on the day I was called up,' he said. 'In Eichstätt. Haven't seen them for over a year.' He looked down to the right, upon the beautiful view of the Plain of Spoleto. 'What a respite,' he said, 'from the deafening barrage of artillery.' Briefly he closed his eyes and I have to admit that my heart went out to him, not to the German officer, but to the man, a doctor thrown into war against his will, longing to be back in Eichstätt with his wife and children and to practise his profession, saving human lives instead of participating in the effort to annihilate part of the human race.

The car halted in front of the Hermitage. The Father Guardian came out and accompanied us on a brief tour of the building. Then, when the brothers gathered for vespers, I took the Colonel along a steep flagged path to the saint's grotto and the grottoes of his companions where they had all lived for some time. I pointed out to him the Tree of the Birds, where our saint used to converse with them, and then we came to the bridge over the dried-up bed of the waterfall, said to have stopped running at his command in order not to disturb the friars' prayers. As we turned back and the breath-taking view of our holy city opened up before us, the Colonel stopped. 'Padre,' he said, 'would you do me the honour of being my father confessor? I haven't been to confession for a long time.' I agreed immediately.

The return journey was much faster and we were soon back at San Damiano, to my brothers' sighs of relief. Once more we alighted from the car and once more we entered the little church, but this time I entered the confessional, the Colonel knelt down and we said our prayers together. Then he began to confess his sins and trespasses. Although all this happened thirty-five years ago, I am not permitted to disclose the details of his confession, but this much I can say—he committed no crime, killed no man, even though it was a war. When he had pledged his penitence and received absolution, I felt that he had ceased to be a German officer and a hated enemy. A close bond was established between us. 'Commandante,' I said, walking him back to his car, 'I can't help feeling that your appointment to Assisi was made not only by the German High Command but perhaps also by God, with the mission willed by Him of protecting our holy shrines and monasteries from the ravages of war.' He said nothing in reply, but his face looked serious and pensive.

Was I being honest? Did I really believe in what I said? Or was I being calculating, and trying to enlist the Colonel's help? It is hard to say. Perhaps both. Before getting into the car, he turned to me. 'Padre, anything I can do to help the Bishop and you and your brothers in your religious tasks, I will do. You can count on me.' His driver started the engine. Müller leaned forward. 'In case I don't see you before, Merry Christmas to you.'

'Merry Christmas,' I said. 'Merry Christmas, Colonello.'

X

It was a good Christmas. Colonel Müller ordered the release of extra rations for the people of Assisi and sent cases of Rhine and Moselle wine to the Bishop, the rectors and the father guardians. He endeared himself quickly to the local inhabitants not so much by his generosity as by his daily afternoon strolls through the city, when he would mingle with the people, listening to their problems and trying to help whenever he could. The day after Christmas was a Sunday, and I was just taking a seat at the Minerva when I saw Colonel Müller walking, all by himself, across the piazza towards me. He saluted me with enthusiasm, snapped his fingers at Renzi, calling for wine and a chess set, and sat at my table as if he and not Luigi had arranged to meet me for a game. I thanked him for the Christmas present and he, in a jovial, festive mood, waved his hand. 'It's nothing, really nothing.'

We started the game. I didn't have much chance, not only because I was no match for him, but also because all eyes were on us, including those of Luigi, who came quietly in, sat at a distant table and gazed at me anxiously as if fearing that I was about to betray his role in the underground. When I finished my wine, the Colonel pushed his own untouched glass towards me. 'It's no Moselle,' I said.

'No,' he smiled. 'It isn't.'

There was a sudden burst of music. A three-man orchestra dressed like opera buffa artists, in splendid uniforms, wearing long red shoes with upturned toes, sounded introductory chords on their trumpet, violin and cymbals. The fattest of them raised a hand-made megaphone to his mouth and, like a town crier, announced an early evening concert of Neapolitan songs.

The Colonel became engrossed in 'Torna a Sorrento', the first song on the programme, and turned from the game. I uttered my private thanks to heaven. At last we felt safe from persecution and razzias. In the week preceding the holiday, we had boldly legitimised the presence of most of our charges in town. All those who neither looked Jewish nor had an accent presented themselves at the Casa del Comune and obtained proper residence permits and food coupons, just like other refugees from the south, their new documents bearing a city stamp stating 'proveniente da terra occupata dal nemico', 'coming from enemy-occupied territory'. And so we were able to share our Christmas Eve dinner and the Colonel's wine with our Jewish flock not in the cloisters but in the dining-rooms of the sisters' guest-houses.

Müller now again looked at the chess board and made his move, checking my king. My situation was hopeless and I surrendered. The Colonel got up. 'You are always welcome', he said, 'to a return game at the Hotel Subasio. Together with a glass or two of Moselle.'

He saluted and left and no one in the cafe seemed to mind my keeping the German's company. 'Buon uomo,' they kept saying, 'questo nuovo Commandante della Piazza,' and their smiles betrayed an eagerness to keep him in charge of the city until the very end of the war.

In the last days of December we set up two clandestine schools in Assisi. One, at the Laboratorio di San Francesco, was run by Don Brunacci, who had collected together trusted clerics with teaching experience so that the Jewish youngsters would not lose a year because of the German occupation. The other, under my direction, consisted of courses on how to behave as Christians in order not to arouse suspicion. If the refugees were to walk in the streets of Assisi they also had to attend church, and so I conducted a special seminar on catechism and liturgy. I remember one day, when crossing the Piazza San Rufino, I was greeted by a cheerful 'Buongiorno, Padre Rufino'. I saw two pretty girls, neatly dressed, breviaries in their hands, black shawls over their heads. It took me a moment to realise that they were the daughters of Professor Viterbi. 'We are going to the Cathedral,' the younger girl, Miriam, said. 'For mass.'

I had not seen them in my class. 'Do you know', I asked in a worried whisper, 'what to do there?'

'Certainly, Padre,' Graziella smiled. 'Some of our best friends at school, in Padua, were Catholics.'

Perhaps the most daring of all was Giorgio Kropf. He had made for himself visiting cards reading: 'Giorgio Cianura, commerciante. Via del Perrone 5, Catanzaro', and had gone into business with, of all people, the pharmacist Pietro Cogolli, the Fascist, supplying him with medicines, which he managed to obtain from God knows where. And because of his successful commercial activities he was soon able to afford to take out his sweetheart, Hella Gelb. I often saw the two of them at the Excelsior, enjoying their coffee and exchanging greetings with Cogolli, Mayor Checconi and Marshal Vivo.

Hella's sister, Deborah, soon became Assisi's leading religious artist. Her paintings, depicting scenes from our saints' lives were fetching high prices from eager German Catholic tourists. Yet she was not allowed to take out her boy-friend because Pali Jozsa, a Yugoslav, had a heavy accent, and so their romance had to grow in the monastery under the watchful eyes of the nuns.

And how right I was to have forbidden all those with an accent or Jewish features to leave the convent. Old Jacob Baruch was unfortunately blessed with both. On one cool but sunny day he stepped out onto the pavement, just outside San Quirico, after looking through the spy-hole and making sure that no one was in sight. But suddenly a German soldier roared out of a side street on his motocycle. Terrified, Baruch scurried into the church, losing his skull-cap in his hurry. He rushed to the altar, knelt and buried his head in his hands, listening with growing alarm to the approaching sound of army boots. 'You lost your zucchetto, Padre,' he heard the soldier's voice and saw his hat being held out in front of him. In the almost complete darkness of the church, the German did not notice that the old man wore civilian clothes. After that incident, never again did Jacob Baruch venture, even for a second, beyond the convent walls.

On New Year's Day I was walking across the Piazza Santa Chiara when the young sacristan of Santa Maria Maggiore came towards me from the Via San Agnese. 'I was just going to fetch you, Padre,' he said. 'His Excellency, the Lord Bishop would like to see you.'

I was sure that Nicolini wanted to offer me a glass of wine and to wish me a happy new year, as he always did, and I looked forward to meeting many friends at his palace. In a happy mood, I walked down to the Piazza del Vescovado. Emilia opened the gate, and the sacristan left me. But as I walked up the stairs I heard no sound of guests and when I reached the reception room no wine stood on the table. Nicolini sat gravely on the sofa, all alone in the huge room. 'Sit down, Padre,' he said, pointing to a chair. 'I have a very important matter to discuss with you.'

I made my obeisance and sat opposite him. The Bishop, even in the gravest of circumstances, usually had a twinkle in his eye. But not today. 'Padre Rufino,' he said, 'the

Cardinal wants you to take a group of people to Abruzzi.'

I jumped to my feet. 'Not me! Cardinal della Costa said he had special volunteers for the task.'

'He had. They were caught, south of Rome. He now wants to try another route. There is a lot of traffic across the Sangro river. No smuggler has ever been caught there. The Cardinal has already collected together the first group.'

'Monsignore!' I cried out in anguish. 'They are not even *our* Jews!'

The Bishop waved at the roof of a legnaia, visible in the window. 'Yes, they are, now. They arrived here last night.'

I walked nervously across the room and looked down at the large oblong building on the other side of the garden where wood was stored for the winter and where the Jews from Florence had been housed. 'Can't I hide them here, in Assisi? It's probably the safest place in Italy.'

'Today, yes. But what about tomorrow? And even if it continues to be safe, how many could we shelter here? Padre Rufino, there are over forty thousand Jews in Italy needing our help. And they are all *our* Jews, and all of us are responsible for their fate.'

I still tried to protest. 'Your Excellency, I'm not a smuggler. I am a priest and a monk.'

'You won't have to help them across the frontier. In Pescocostanzo the professional smugglers will take over.'

'Are the trains running to Abruzzi?'

'No, you'll have to go by road.'

'How?'

He shrugged as if to underline that this was the easiest of the problems. 'Contact Trasporti di Gregori of Foligno. They're active in the underground. They'll provide a truck.'

'Monsignore! The Germans check trucks at least once or twice on a journey. Especially on the road to the front, they would stop us a dozen times.'

'That's exactly why the Cardinal chose you. You are very good at confronting the Germans.' For the first time the twinkle came back into his eyes. 'Apparently you are now not only my uomo di fiducia but also the Cardinal's.'

'Thank you,' I said tartly. 'Thank you very much. It's not just this one assignment, Monsignore. It's not that I'm frightened, though I am. It's that if something should happen to me hundreds of people who depend on me will be lost.'

'Yes, but if things become unbearable in Assisi, and they are already unbearable in the rest of Italy under the Nazis, you may not be able to help them anyway.' He heaved his short, bulky body off the sofa and joined me at the window. 'There are fifteen of them there, including a rabbi. Remember, in the first group you took to Florence, there was also a rabbi. His holy scroll is under my bed, awaiting his return after the war. It was thanks to you that he managed to get abroad. But now we must open a new escape route. We must keep one step ahead of the Nazis. I don't have to tell you what the alternative could be.' Reassuringly, he patted my shoulder. 'May I notify His Eminence that he was right in putting his trust in you?' I do not doubt that the Bishop had known, even before I did, that no matter how torn I was inside I would eventually comply with the wishes of my superiors. 'By the way,' he added, smiling, 'they all have proper documents, prepared by your own "passport office". There are three priests among them, including a monsignore— the rabbi, of course.' As I knelt down to kiss the episcopal ring, my eyes were focused on the floor to hide my reluctance. The Lord Bishop helped me up. 'I didn't hold a reception this year, as there is nothing to celebrate and no wine left, despite the Colonel's gift. But I can still manage a glass of Santa Giustina for you. Will you have some?'

'Thank you, Monsignore, but I really don't feel like wine just now.' He stared at me as I walked across the reception room to the door. It was the first time he had ever heard me refuse a drink.

I returned to San Damiano shortly after the noon prayers and I was glad that the church was empty. In my favourite chapel I knelt before the 300-year-old crucifix and prayed for guidance. Four months had passed since I had become involved in the underground. I had had moments of fear, but in the mornings I tried not to think of the restless nights and my occasional nightmares. With the arrival of Colonel Müller, peace and tranquillity seemed to have finally returned to Assisi, but this new assignment jolted me out of a false sense of security.

What worried me most about the plan was the journey itself. There were numerous checkpoints on the road, as I knew from Battaglia and the refugees who scaled the mountains to avoid them. It was enough for one German soldier or an OVRA man at one of them to become suspicious and we would all be lost. I had to alter the plan, to make the journey safe. I stopped praying, but remained on my knees, my head buried in my hands, all kinds of ideas going through it. I raised my eyes to Christ's face, but His silent gaze did not convey to me any hope. He seemed to be suffering with me.

But suddenly I realised that I was kneeling at the right-hand side of the statue and I moved over to the left side. I had forgotten that the '*Christ on the Crucifix*' by Innocenzo da Palermo had different sides to his face. And now when I raised my head and saw that he was smiling at me, I smiled back. Call it a miracle if you wish, but it was at that moment that I hit upon an idea, daring and yet simple.

I am a man of action. The moment I decide to do something, I do it. And so I did not even stop to inquire how my brothers were enjoying their holiday, but returned to the city—and to Colonel Müller's office. Hadn't he invited me for a game of chess and a glass of Moselle? And what better time to bring him my best wishes than on New Year's Day?

At the Hotel Subasio the atmosphere had changed. There were no German soldiers in sight drinking schnapps. Two young medical officers sat in the lobby drinking coffee, their heads bent over a map of the city. From behind the desk Signor Rossi greeted me with a 'Buon anno' and I waved to him and replied with 'Tanti auguri'. An unarmed soldier sat outside the Stadtkommissar's office. As I approached, he got up and I told him that the Colonel had invited me. A moment later, through the half-open door, I saw Müller himself rising from behind his desk and walking towards me with an outstretched hand. 'Come in, Padre Rufino! How good of you to come.' The door closed behind us, but not before the Colonel had raised his forefinger and uttered a magic word, 'Moselle'. He had not forgotten.

I expressed my own best wishes and those of my brothers, and of the whole city. Müller smiled with satisfaction, then he wished me, the clergy, and Assisi's inhabitants all the best on behalf of himself and the German Army. The wine was brought in and the Colonel himself filled the glasses to the brim. 'Cin cin!' he said. 'Buon anno!' I responded. We drank the toast. 'I am really glad you came,' he said. He waved apologetically towards the desk. 'Even on a holiday I have a lot of work. Every day our wounded are arriving by the dozen and Sunday is no exception. We are running out of hospitals and even schools converted into hospitals. And your hotels and public buildings are being used as convalescent centres. He sighed. 'Have you ever seen men with their legs or hands blown off, or faces burnt beyond recognition?'

'No,' I said. 'Perhaps I should come later.' I rose from my chair.

'Oh, no, I also need a moment to rest.' From a drawer he pulled out a box. 'Let's have a game. I owe you one, remember?' It was a small box of oriental design. He opened it and little filigree chessmen fell on the desk. We set them up on the board and as I had white I made the first move. He quickly replied by advancing his pawn. 'If you hadn't come, I would probably have played by myself. I often do that, solve problems or imitate famous games from a chess magazine. Next to prayers, I find chess most relaxing.'

I took another drink. 'Excellent wine!' I complimented my host. 'Excellent!'

'Before you leave,' he said matter-of-factly, 'I will have a few bottles wrapped up for you, Padre.'

'Colonel, what I came for, apart from bringing my best wishes, was to ask for your help. You once told me not to hesitate if there was anything I needed.'

'But of course.'

'A group of pilgrims from Pescocostanzo are stranded here. They came to celebrate Christmas. But no trains are running to Abruzzi and we cannot obtain any vehicle for them. Would it be imposing if I asked you, Colonel, whether you could help us with a truck? His Excellency the Lord Bishop joins me in this request. There are a few priests and an important church official, a monsignore, in that group. And I will be going, too, since I have to attend to some ecclesiastical business in Pescocostanzo.'

'I don't see why not,' he answered, making a move. 'I have a few vehicles free. I would like to be of service to the Church, and to you. When would you like to go?'

Thank God! It was as simple as that. The army truck, with a German soldier at the wheel, would just be waved on at a checkpoint. 'In a day or two,' I said.

But my plan worked even beyond my greatest expectations. 'I'll provide you with an escort, a couple of armed soldiers. One never knows—there are partisans, or there could be an Allied ambush. It's near the front line, isn't it?'

'Yes. Naturally it would be better to have an army escort. Thank you, Colonel, thank you very much.'

'Not at all, not at all. Your move, Padre.'

I was elated. I would rather have the German Army than Gregori of Foligno work for my underground. We drank the whole bottle and then, true to his word, Colonel Müller had three bottles wrapped up for me. I lost the game, of course, but that did not matter, it did not matter at all.

I hurried through the narrow, winding streets of Assisi back to the Palazzo del Vescovado, eager to boast of my accomplishment. Just at the entrance to the piazza, there was a poster on the wall of Mussolini proclaiming with a raised hand: 'No one but God can break the Fascist will.' Perhaps I was a little drunk, unaccustomed to undiluted wine; perhaps I had just regained my old self-confidence. But I pulled out a pencil, glanced over my shoulder and then quickly scrawled on the poster: 'We place our trust in God!' Chuckling inwardly, I knocked at the gate. As usual, Emilia opened it. I left my package on the chair in the corridor downstairs and climbed up, only to meet Nicolini himself at the top of the stairs. He was just on his way down. 'I've got good news!' I exclaimed and told him about Müller's offer.

The Bishop jubilantly clapped me on the back. 'Wasn't I right', he said, 'in leaving all the details of the arrangements to you? I knew you would find a way. Come and meet your charges.'

We walked across the big garden to the legnaia. The Bishop

led me through rooms stacked with old furniture to a big hall filled with sacks of coal and wood stored for the winter. From behind a wall of logs a man's face emerged; frightened eyes scrutinised us. 'It's the Bishop,' I heard the man say in a reassuring voice. A few of the men had already rushed to the back door, leading to an open field. The three 'priests' sat together on a bench and I could not stop myself from greeting them with a bow and the sign of the cross. The 'monsignore' was a corpulent man in his fifties, appropriately dressed in a distinctive reddish-blue cassock, with a pectoral cross and another one engraved on his ring. The Bishop introduced me and then I described our forthcoming journey to Pescocostanzo. They were taken aback by the idea of going in a German truck under the protection of German soldiers. The rabbi explained that many of them had seen their families for the last time in exactly such circumstances. I had to persuade them that in our particular case this was the safest way to reach our destination.

Slowly the feeling of gloom gave way to a more optimistic mood, as I managed to reassure them by my words and the Bishop's obvious trust in me. We even joked a bit, and they laughed when I told them what I had written on the Mussolini poster.

'We always say in our prayers,' the rabbi said, '"Next year in Jerusalem!" Who knows, maybe this "next year" has just arrived.'

As we talked, I was delighted to discover that the rabbi used broad pastoral gestures, probably ingrained in him through the years of preaching from the synagogue pulpit. They matched his attire perfectly. I asked the people to show me their identity documents. After all, I was an official of the 'passport office'. I joked. They were beautiful. Brizi was doing a superb job. 'You know,' Nicolini turned to me with a chuckle, 'I was told by Brunacci, who has just returned from Rome, that they are fetching a high price there on the black market. I bet if you and Brizi set out to forge a Leonardo you would both make a fortune.'

Nicolini returned to the palace. In the corridor I picked up my parcel. I must really have been drunk, because in a sudden outburst of generosity I offered a bottle to the Bishop. 'For you, Excellency,' I said. 'With my best wishes.'

'Thank you, Padre Rufino,' he answered and then on the spur of the moment added, 'Let's share the wine with our fellow men, eh? After all, it's their New Year as much as ours.' And he turned round.

I was about to protest that they had already celebrated their New Year in September, but I did not want to embarrass the Bishop. I put my parcel back on the chair and was about to follow him.

'Oh, no!' he exclaimed, turning to me in the door. 'Take all the wine with you. What's one bottle for seventeen people? Emilia! Bring plenty of glasses to the legnaia! Quick!'

Ruefully, I picked up my parcel and followed our Lord Bishop to drink a New Year's toast with our Jewish brothers, compliments of the German Stadtkommissar of Assisi.

XI

The canvas-covered German army truck stopped in front of the Vescovado. Beside the driver sat a corporal, and in the back of the vehicle were two soldiers, guns slung across their backs.

I was standing waiting for them on the pavement. As soon as the truck came to a halt, I said, 'Un momento' and raised my hand, trusting that my gesture would make it more clear to them than my Italian that my companions would be coming down in a moment. I called and shortly afterwards they trooped out from the Bishop's quarters, where they had spent the night being entertained by Nicolini in the best way he could manage. He himself followed them down, to add authority by his presence. I was filled with admiration for his acting ability, especially when he put his arms around the 'monsignore' in a fraternal priestly embrace. When I recall that touching farewell, I think that perhaps the main reason why we succeeded where others failed was that we Italians, whether peasants, merchants or priests, are born actors. We are all, by tradition and temperament, students of the *commedia dell'arte*, great followers of the art of improvisation.

The German soldiers seemed as happy as Colonel Müller to be of service to us. The corporal respectfully beckoned to the 'monsignore' to take the honoured place in the cab, next to the driver. The Bishop, who spoke German, coming as he did from the Alto Adige near the Austrian border, had to persuade the soldier that it was I who was leading the group and knew the directions. And so the corporal made me take his place.

A black Mercedes drove quickly into the piazza and Colonel Müller alighted from it, saluting the Bishop and myself. He had come, he said, to ascertain for himself that everything had been arranged to our satisfaction. He went to the rear of the truck, inspected the passengers, shook hands with the rabbi, wished us all a happy journey, and then waved to the driver to start.

And off we went. We rumbled past the women with their shopping bags, the old men staring at us from the cafés, and a group of black-robed seminarists on their way to the basilica. Through the Porta Nuova we reached the main highway and joined the other German trucks driving south.

The driver tried to start a conversation, but I could not understand a single word he said. Suddenly he clapped his forehead in a gesture indicating that he had found a common language and from under his seat pulled out a straw-wrapped bottle of Chianti. I shook my head—I had to keep it clear—and the man, disappointed, put the bottle back. We were approaching Foligno and then I saw in front of me the first German checkpoint. I patted my pocket to ascertain that the Bishop's letter was safely there. But ours was only one of many trucks blocking the road, and the military policeman impatiently waved all the vehicles on, anxious to keep the traffic moving. He did not cast so much as a glance at us. The same thing happened near Spoleto and Terni, but once we turned off the highway leading towards Rome I noticed suddenly that there were not many German vehicles around.

After a while the driver looked at me and gestured towards his open mouth. 'Essen,' he said. 'Mangiare.' This one Italian word he knew. No doubt he knew a couple of others, like vino, signorina. 'L'Aquila,' he added. This was the name of the big town on the way to Abruzzi. I nodded, uttering, 'Grazie.' It was just then that I noticed another checkpoint. There were no vehicles in front or behind us. I quickly pulled out my rosary and began to pray. The soldier looked at me curiously. 'Nona,' I said in Italian. 'The canonical hour. The hour when Christ died.' The soldier shook his head, but smiled.

I could see the German military policeman waving us to a stop. The driver switched into second gear, then first, then halted the truck. The German soldier approached us, followed by an OVRA man. In response to a question, the driver took out a letter. Silently I blessed the Colonel; he had thought of everything. Meanwhile the OVRA man, eager to show that he also had his job to do, came to my side of the truck. 'Buongiorno, Padre,' he said. 'Dove andate?' 'A Pescocostanzo,' I answered and pulled out the Bishop's letter. But the Italian had not even time to start reading it. 'Alles ist in Ordnung,' the German soldier said with a tone of authority and he waved us on.

We reached L'Aquila. We had been travelling several hours and were hungry and eager to stretch our legs. The truck halted in front of a café-restaurant and we all got out. The place was almost empty, as it was already past the lunch hour. The owner, a rotund, bald man, raised his hand in the Fascist salute and snapped his fingers to summon his three waiters. They moved the tables into one long line, covered them with checked tablecloths and then suggested we go to the kitchen to look into the pans and sample the food. We, Italians, did just that, but when we returned, having ordered cannelloni and pasta, the Germans were opening some cans that they had brought along. I had never seen canned meat before. The soldiers asked the owner to heat up their corned beef and sausages. The corporal, I noticed, was effusively courteous to the 'monsignore', seating him at the head of the table and filling his glass with good white Trebbiano, which was brought up from the restaurant's cellar. Through the window we could see the mountains, and the owner, with great pride, explained to us that we were looking at Gran Sasso d'Italia where the Duce, who had been imprisoned by Badoglio, was whisked away from the Campo Imperatore by airborne commandoes. We all nodded in sheer admiration at the exploit and then concentrated on our meal. The corporal was surprised by the refusal of the 'monsignore' to share the soldiers' food. But to make up for him, I ate several of the pork sausages with gusto, washing them down with a little wine. I still had to keep a cool head.

Suddenly, as we were finishing our meal, the window pane became blurred. It was raining outside, then lightning struck, followed by distant thunder. 'We'd better wait until the storm is over,' the Corporal said. At least that is what I understood him to say, pointing at the window and waving happily at the wine on the table. But my head was clear.

'No,' I answered, 'we'd better go. At five it will be dark and we still have a hundred or more kilometres to cover.' What I really hoped for was that, as we approached the front line checkpoints, the soldiers would wave us on because of the rain. Reluctantly, the corporal agreed. We offered to pay, but he would not hear of it. The Colonel, he explained, had provided him with money to pay for our meal.

We ran through the rain and climbed aboard the vehicle again. After an hour or so, I discovered that not only was the rain helping us, but also that there were German trucks carrying ammunition and supplies around us once more. We were getting nearer to the front and the sounds of artillery shells became audible. The checkpoints became more frequent, but still the German soldiers waved us on. Finally we could make out the contours of tall buildings and the towering campaniles of churches. We were entering the suburbs of Pescocostanzo, only thirteen kilometres from the River Sangro and from the Allied troops on the other side.

We stopped once or twice to ask the way. The streets were almost deserted and the rain had now settled into a quiet drizzle. The chimes of church bells gave an undertone of peace to the sporadic sounds of gunfire. At last we reached the southern end of the city and halted in front of a small church. I had barely stepped down from the truck when I saw a short perspiring man with an umbrella rushing out of the church. I didn't have to ask who he was, as he grabbed my hand, pumping it warmly. 'In time for vespers,' he said with delight.

The others climbed out of the truck with their suitcases and bundles. The German soldiers helped the three 'priests' with their luggage. On the church steps the Italians began shaking hands with the Germans, exchanging 'grazie's for their 'bitte schön's. The corporal spoke to me and raised six fingers. I nodded. They would spend the night at a nearby army camp and pick me up at six o'clock in the morning. The soldiers took their places in the back and the driver at the wheel. And then something unexpected happened. Just before climbing in next to the driver, the corporal turned round, bent his knee, grabbed the hand of the 'monsignore' and kissed his ring. I held my breath, but the rabbi was equal to the occasion. His face became solemn. 'Ti benedico, in nome del Padre, del Figlio e dello Spirito Santo,' he recited and made the sign of the cross over the Catholic corporal.

The man jumped into the truck and drove off. 'Come inside!' Don Paolo exclaimed. 'Do you want to catch cold?'

The portly priest led us to a reception room, where a little meal was awaiting us at a white-clothed table. He sat next to me and passed gnocchi and polenta around, then said we should help ourselves to wine. 'It's all arranged,' he said happily.

'Good.'

'Luigi will be here shortly.'

'The smuggler?'

'Yes. A friendly man.'

We sat in semi-darkness until a black-kerchiefed woman brought an oil lamp. Don Paolo explained: 'The electricity went off yesterday, when an Allied shell hit the power station.' He smiled. 'Good for you. It ought to be easier to get to the mountains and cross the river.'

A small, thin man appeared in the door, twisting a peaked cap in his hand. Don Paolo quickly jumped from his chair. 'Oh, Luigi, come in.' He introduced us. The smuggler was a man in his forties with a weather-beaten face and small eyes. He was constantly chewing tobacco. 'Sit down,' Don Paolo said cordially to his guest, pushing a chair towards him. 'Have some gnocchi with us.' The man shook his head. The priest filled a glass with wine. Luigi took it and sipped it slowly, all the while continuing to chew his tobacco. We all sat silent, our eyes focused on him. When finally he put the glass down, he looked at the window, murky with rain. 'It's snowing in the mountains,' he said. I nodded. 'We leave at nine. You have the money?'

'Yes, of course.' I made no move.

'Pay.'

I glanced uneasily at Don Paolo. 'It's all right,' the smugglers' priest said. 'You can trust Luigi.'

I dug the banknotes out of the inner pocket of my habit. The smuggler counted them slowly, licking his fingers. Then he put the money on the table. 'It's not enough,' he said.

'What? Signor Battaglia made the arrangements. Two hundred lire per person. There are three thousand here. Count again.'

'Luigi,' Don Paolo interceded nervously, 'this is what you agreed on.'

'It's snowing,' the man said. 'I didn't know it would be snowing.'

'What difference does it make?'

'It will stop snowing in an hour or two. Footsteps will be visible. The danger is much greater.'

I threw up my hands in anguish. 'But we haven't got any more money.'

Luigi got up. 'Then wait a few days until the snow melts into mud. Then it's only two hundred per person.' Without a word, he picked up his cap and started towards the door. As everyone in the room looked at each other in despair, Don Paolo rushed after the smuggler. I heard him pleading with him, offering him two absolutions in advance. But the man just kept shaking his head. Then he said, 'I am not alone in this, you know that, Padre. Vittorio wants double.'

I joined the two at the door. In the church, lit by hanging oil lamps and burning tapers, I could see people gathering for vespers. 'Signor Luigi,' I said, 'the Holy See, our Cardinal, our Bishop, they will all bless you.'

'It doesn't help when you are shot.'

'But you're going across the river anyway, aren't you?'

'For smuggling merchandise the penalty is prison. For taking people to the Allied side it's execution.' He waved a salute to someone in the church. 'My mother and wife have just come in. I must join them. I'll see you after vespers. But you'd better have six thousand lire ready.' And he left.

I turned to Don Paolo, asking him to plead with the smuggler, but it was no use. Both the men, Vittorio and Luigi, were as stubborn, he said, as their mules. 'Wouldn't they at least consent to give me credit? I'd get the money to them in a few days.

Again the smugglers' priest shook his head. 'It's cash only,' he said. 'No credit. I know my men.'

The rabbi joined us at the door. I had not even been aware that while Don Paolo and I had been talking to Luigi the group had been busy. 'Here,' the Rabbi handed me a bundle, 'it's all we have, eight hundred and twenty lire.'

'Well,' I said, 'that's something.' I looked glumly at the people gathering in the church for vespers, most of them carrying umbrellas. 'There is only one thing for us to do,' I decided. 'Let us take a church collection.'

'You're not going to tell them what it's for?' Don Paolo asked wearily.

'I'll tell them it's for the poor and destitute war refugees. For our patron saint's good work.'

Don Paolo clasped my arm. 'Good idea. Sit at the altar when I conduct the prayers and then you'll deliver the sermon and we shall pass the hat—and pray.'

Our 'priests' and the civilians joined the others in the church. I gave them all their money back, so that they could show an example by their generosity. The three 'priests', of course, sat in the front pew. Don Paolo and I put on white albs and red chasubles and with the help of the choirboys, who carried a monstrance and a chalice from the sacristy, Don Paolo said the prayers. Wisely, he conducted a low mass, to speed up matters, and then he called me to the pulpit. I was in good form. I spoke about the war and the refugees and the meagre food rations, children stricken with scurvy, and nursing mothers with no milk in their breasts. I noticed the impassive face of Luigi in the third pew, his two women on one side, and another man on his right, a bit older, whom I imagined to be his partner, Vittorio. Then the boys passed round, asking for donations. They approached our party, who gave what they had. The rest of the congregation followed suit. Luigi, still without the slightest change of expression, gave too. And Vittorio and his family added some lire as well. They have always been a generous people, the Italians, especially in church and for a worthwhile cause.

As the people started to leave and the sacristan began extinguishing the tapers, Don Paolo and I rushed to the reception room to count the money. We had 2,600 lire. We were still 400 short.

Don Paolo smiled at me reassuringly. I saw him dashing back to the church, to an alms box. He emptied it and rushed back to me. It took us a while to count all the small coins, but there, finally, we had the sum we needed—even a few lire to spare. Thus when Luigi and Vittorio, their caps in their hands, entered the room, we were happy to announce that the people of Pescocostanzo had performed their greatest act of Christian piety—that of charity towards their fellow men.

'Good,' Luigi said, and the stocky, barrel-chested Vittorio helped himself to a glass of wine from an almost empty carafe. 'I have eight children to feed,' he said. 'And Luigi has six.' That was all he said, and I think I understood him, especially when he added with a sigh, 'Noi poveri Italiani—we poor Italians.'

It was a time-honoured saying which explained everything. The misery of tilling an arid land, one meal a day for peasants and the unemployed, the mass emigration of Italians—as well as to Vittorio's eight children and Luigi's six.

It was still raining when we left the church. The town lay in total darkness, and it was only by the flickering light of oil lamps shining through the wooden shutters that we were able to grope our way along the gravel road to a grove of olive trees. There, hidden in the shadows of their gnarled branches, stood a camioncino, a wartime Italian invention that ingeniously converted a motorcycle into a three-wheeled truck. I went along with the group. I could not let them go the last thirteen kilometres alone and I also felt that I had to know the route that we were, we hoped, to follow again in similar operations. Vittorio sat in front, next to Luigi, who was driving. They not only knew the back paths leading to the Sangro, they also had arms hidden under their seats. And so, swaying dangerously on the benches which had been put under the canvas awning, we set off; and it must have been one of St Francis's miracles that our camioncino, with its heavy throbbing and chugging, did not wake up the whole city and arouse the attention of the German guards patrolling the streets.

We drove for a long time, with dimmed headlamps lighting our way through the rain. The vehicle kept swerving from the narrow road and skidding on the mud, throwing us against one another. The night air was steadily growing colder as we climbed higher and soon the knotted oaks gave way to tall gleaming pines. Suddenly the silver curtain of rain behind us turned to white. It was snowing. And I started to pray again—that Luigi would turn out to have been wrong and that it would keep snowing all through the night. Frosty gusts of wind began to blow from the mountain top and we huddled together as closely as possible for warmth.

But Luigi knew his mountains, his weather and his job only too well. When we finally halted in a small clearing in the forest, with the road going no further, the ground around us was all covered with a white blanket, but the white flakes had stopped falling, unveiling a portion of sky with a few pale stars. Luigi came round to the back of the truck, a hunting rifle slung across his shoulder. 'Jump down,' he said. One by one, we clambered from the truck, and as we did so we saw a hut. A lonely hut perched over a ravine, its thatched roof and wooden walls covered with heavy snow, a light flickering in its frosted window-pane. A man's face appeared next to the light, eyes peering out. Then both face and light disappeared, the door was flung open and in the light of a lantern held high I saw a white-haired man with a withered face but a surprisingly hard and muscular body. Luigi introduced him: 'Francesco, the forester.' He never said much, Luigi. The smugglers shook hands with the man. 'Come in,' Luigi motioned to us.

We all entered. The hut was warm with pine logs crackling in the fireplace. The entire furnishing consisted of an iron bed under a picture of the Madonna on the wall, a tall cupboard, a large chest and a heavy rough-hewn table with two benches. There was the smell of something cooking on a primus in the corner. Luigi turned to us. 'We eat, then go.'

The forester put the pot on the table and then at random handed a few of us some thick wooden spoons. 'Risi e bisi,' he said with pride. We ate our rice and beans direct from the pot and when the first group had finished, they passed on their spoons to the others. We washed the food down with a few mouthfuls of hot barley coffee, surprisingly sweet. The forester pointed at Luigi. 'French sugar.'

'Are the French on the other side of the Sangro?' I asked.

Luigi nodded. Then he beckoned to me and I followed him out. We came to the edge of the ravine. Down below, a kilometre or two away, I could see a pale bluish ribbon of water, hardly visible in the night. 'The Sangro,' he said. 'We have two boats hidden in a cave. We shall cross the river twice, to get everybody to the other side.' I saw a few lights shimmering in a valley down to our right.

'Ateleto,' Luigi said, noticing my look. 'The Germans are there.' Then, instead of returning to the hut, he went further into the forest. A moment later he reappeared, leading two mules by their bridles. 'For carrying the merchandise back,' he explained. 'We will be back in a few hours. You wait up here, Padre.' He walked to the door. 'Time to go!'

I embraced all my charges. 'Come to Assisi after the war,' I said.

'We shall!' And the rabbi added, 'God willing.' Then he took a long look down the steep forest path leading to the river, and then down they went, led by Luigi, with Vittorio in the rear, both of them carrying their guns and leading their mules. The tracks of the people and animals were visible in the fresh snow. I looked at old Francesco. His pale, thin lips were moving in words of prayer.

The old man put out a cot for me and handed me a worn out blanket. I lay down, while Francesco sat at the fireplace, lit a long-stemmed wooden pipe and kept vigil, staring at the glowing embers. 'It's quiet tonight,' he said. 'No guns. Too cold and windy for war.'

'Is it profitable, the business?'

'Oh, yes. The Allies have everything. Sugar and salt and even coffee and cigarettes. We have nothing.'

'Have any of the smugglers ever been caught?'

'No,' he said. He glanced at the window. 'The night is good.

Dark and cold. The snow is bad, but the night is good. Sleep, Padre. It will be a few hours before they return. And when they do, we will have to go down.'

'What for?'

'To help load the animals. You are young and strong, Padre. We're helping you, you'll help us.'

'How will you know when they are back?'

'A shot,' he said. 'A single shot from our man on the other side of the river. Germans pay no attention to it. And now sleep. We have hard work ahead of us.'

I lapsed into an uneasy doze. Once when I woke up, I saw Francesco on his bed, fully clothed, snoring. It was the most reassuring sound that night. If he could sleep, so could I—and I fell back into a sort of numbed stupor. It was the rifle shot that awoke me again. I smiled. They are back, I thought. Francesco sat up on his bed. But then other shots followed and suddenly Schmeissers and Spandaus opened up. 'My God!' I exclaimed. 'They must have been caught!'

The old man crossed himself and then fell to his knees in front of the picture of the Madonna. Without a word I joined him. But then I saw him halt in the middle of his Ave Maria. He rushed to the door and flung it open. Tracers of machine-gun fire appeared, coming from across the river, and then bursts of artillery broke out. Francesco smiled happily, grabbed his pipe, filled it and lit it.

'The Germans probably caught a French patrol, and now the Allies are giving artillery support to help them extricate themselves. Good, they are too busy fighting each other to pay any attention to us! You want some wine, Father?'

'Yes,' I said. 'But you didn't finish your prayers.'

'God understands.' And he went to the cupboard and brought back a bottle of red country wine and two glasses. 'They will come soon,' he said, pouring the wine. 'The Allies. The Germans have already mined all the public buildings in Pescocostanzo.'

'And then the business will end,' I said.

'So it will. And so will the killing.'

Suddenly, against the rat-tat-tat of machine-guns and automatic fire and sporadic artillery shells, I heard a shot. A single rifle shot. 'Drink up,' Francesco said, 'and let's go.'

It took us barely ten minutes to get down, and there they were—Luigi, Vittorio and two boats filled with packages, sacks and barrels. 'Safe?' I asked.

Luigi smiled. 'Safe and sound—on the other side of the river. We did our job well. And we bought a lot of merchandise. We had more money to spend. Come, quickly, help! We mustn't waste any time.'

The mules were some fifty metres away. The river bank was slippery and muddy, and the animals would not come to the water.

I don't remember ever working so hard physically as that night. As a boy, I had helped my parents at the mill, carrying sacks of flour. But the seminaries and the monastic life had softened me. I carried sacks, barrels of oil, and large cartons of cigarettes marked 'NAAFI'. When the mules were laden and all the merchandise was fastened to their backs, we started the slow trek up the mountain. It took us over an hour to get to the top. Still gasping from the effort of climbing, I was once more put to work, to tear off or obliterate the 'NAAFI' labelling, as we had to transfer all but Francesco's share of the goods to the truck. Then Vittorio and Luigi took their mules back to their shed. The moon now came out from behind a cloud and I could see the shack, with the picture of the Bambino[1] and, for extra insurance, the pagan ram's horn too nailed to its gate. We shook hands with the old forester. 'See you next week,' Luigi said.

We drove down much faster. It was about five o'clock when the white houses of Pescocostanzo loomed under the pale moonlight. The camioncino halted at the very spot from which we had departed. I jumped down from the vehicle and met Luigi half-way. 'Grazie, Luigi!' I said.

But he didn't answer. He picked up a small barrel of oil from the back of the truck. I saw Vittorio throw a bag of sugar over his shoulder and pick up a sack of salt. They carried their load to the room where I had first met Luigi. Now the smuggler grabbed my hand and shook it. 'See you soon again,' he

---

[1] The Nativity—literally 'The Child'.

said. 'Remember, two hundred lire per head if there's no snow; double if it's snowing.'

'I'll remember,' I said, shaking hands with Vittorio. Luigi, relaxed now, filled his mouth with tobacco. 'This is for Don Paolo,' I said, pointing at the merchandise. 'Right?'

'Oh, no, it's for you. You raised the money, you worked hard, carrying the goods. It's your share, Padre.' And before I could say anything, they were gone.

I slumped into a chair, too tired to sleep. Half an hour later I saw a candlelight and behind it Don Paolo in a long white night-shirt and night-cap. I told him all that had happened, then we made plans for future operations, and while we drank a cup of chicory I heard the sound of a motor horn. 'My German friends,' I said. Ready for the trip home. I walked out.

It was still dark, but I saw the corporal coming towards me. 'Did all go well, Padre?' he asked.

'Very well, thank you. I also obtained some supplies for the poor of Assisi. They are in the church.'

'Good. We shall help you, Padre.' And he ordered his two soldiers to carry the oil, sugar and salt to the truck. The corporal again insisted on my taking a place in the cab. He would sit in the back with his comrades, he said, and guard the stuff. The engine started. Don Paolo, still in his night-shirt, stood at the gate waving to me, and I waved back happily. My mission had been accomplished more successfully than I had anticipated. I had delivered my charges to the Allies, and brought back British supplies under German escort to Jewish refugees.

XII

As our truck turned into the road leading to San Damiano, I could see the reassuring statue of St Clare, her hands protectively raised towards our monastery. But when we were able to see the whole of the building, I became aware that a military

Volkswagen was standing in front of the church. An armed soldier and a civilian were pacing the flagged courtyard as if waiting for somebody. A moment later I realised they were waiting for me.

As soon as I stepped out of the cab, the two men moved forward. The civilian wore a borsalino and dark sun-glasses, the standard 'uniform' of the OVRA agents, who apparently tried to imitate bad characters from bad films and novels. 'Good day, Padre Rufino,' he said, and the soldier behind him added his support by slightly raising his gun. Only now did I notice that we were being watched by a group of worried brothers and fathers gathered in the arcade leading to the inner quarters of the monastery.

'Good day,' I said cheerfully, trying to cover my anxiety.

'Captain von den Velde would like to have a word with you,' the Italian said.

'Captain...?' I looked around. I saw a German officer unhurriedly coming out of the church. He was about forty, tall and slim, with curly blond hair and a small moustache above pale thin lips. Under his arm he carried a baton the way cavalry officers do. But he was not a cavalryman. His black uniform with twin silver flashes on the tunic collar betrayed an SS officer. As I uneasily acknowledged his distant salute, I heard the German corporal in charge of our truck addressing me. 'Where shall we put your provisions, Padre?' It was too late to stop the soldiers carrying the sacks of sugar and salt from the rear of the vehicle. The oil barrel already stood on the ground, a slight golden trickle of liquid oozing out of a tiny hole. 'What's that?' the OVRA man asked, pointing at the barrel.

'Here,' I said to the Corporal. 'You can leave it here.' Then I turned to the Italian. 'Can you see what it is?! It's oil, what else?'

As the Captain approached us, the Corporal saluted quickly, shooed his men into the truck and hurriedly departed, glancing uneasily back at the SS officer.

'I am Captain Ernst von den Velde,' the German said, slowly pronouncing his name. 'From Bastia. In charge of the security of the region.' He spoke Italian, ungrammatically and with a heavy accent, but he spoke it. He waved the soldier and the civilian away.

'Will you come in, Captain,' I said, 'and have a glass of wine?'

'I am German,' he said. 'I don't drink in the morning. How was your trip to Pescocostanzo?'

'Oh, good, thank you. I delivered a group of stranded pilgrims there, attended to some religious business and got a few provisions for our monasteries for the winter.' I knew that he knew and I had to be ahead of him.

He glanced at the barrel and the sacks. 'These provisions', he said pensively watching the liquid ribbon slowly moving towards our feet, 'did not come from the Allied side by any chance? There's not much oil, sugar and salt on this side, I am afraid.'

'The Allied side? How?' I looked stupidly into his face.

'There is a lot of smuggling going on. But you wouldn't participate in such operations, would you? No, of course not, Padre.' He pulled out a heavy silver cigarette case and offered me one. He flicked on a lighter and as we both lit our cigarettes he continued: 'A lot of smuggling—of merchandise and of people. We halted that traffic on the western front in the Apennines and now we are closing the approaches to the River Sangro. Anyway, Padre, as I am new here, I wanted to meet all the lay and religious leaders of the area. I am glad to have made your acquaintance.'

'Good,' I said, relieved. 'Why the hell is no one stopping the hole in that barrel?' I yelled and immediately Padre Vincenzo rushed forward and dug out some newspaper from the inner pocket of his habit and fixed the leak.

The Captain smiled. 'I never heard a monk swear the way you do,' he said.

'Sorry, Captain. I'm a peasant. Can't change my ways. I was already swearing when my mother tried to take my teddy bear away.' I had hoped to ease the tension by making the German laugh, but his face did not move a muscle. They don't have much humour, these Germans.

The OVRA man addressed his superior with eager servility. 'Shouldn't the provisions be confiscated? All civilians have ration coupons entitling them to half a litre of oil a month, 800 grams of pasta...'

'I know,' the Captain interrupted.

'These are for twenty-six monasteries,' I said quickly. 'From the Holy See. They sent it to the Abruzzi diocese and the priests there were generous enough to share some of their supplies with our holy city.'

'Of course,' the Captain said. 'The Italians are very generous people.'

'Where the church is concerned,' I amended his statement, and he managed a kind of smile. The Captain took his seat in the car, the OVRA man got in behind him and the driver started up. At that very moment I thought of Colonel Müller. Undoubtedly von den Velde had his spies on the Stadtkommissar's staff. We must find a contact in the SS in Bastia so that we would be able to keep abreast of their moves.

'Good-day, Padre,' the Captain said. 'And by the way, you have made that trip to Pescocostanzo twice. The first and last time. German army trucks are for transporting troops and war materials, not stranded pilgrims or food for civilians.'

I stared at the Volkswagen until it disappeared from view. The monks now surged forward to greet me. 'Take these inside,' I pointed at the sacks and the barrel. I glanced at my watch. 'Why aren't you attending the nones prayers?' I said. 'Get into the church!'

As soon as they had gone, I set out for town. I had to report to the Bishop and, of course, I had to see the Colonel. But Nicolini was not in. His niece told me that he had gone to Perugia on business and would return late in the afternoon. I told her I would come back then.

Retracing the steps I had taken a few days earlier to see the Bishop after my meeting with Colonel Müller, I walked gloomily back to the Stadtkommissar's headquarters in the Hotel Subasio. Signor Andrea Rossi, the portly hotel owner, was at the reception desk, and the lounge was swarming with officers. They were all medical officers, I noticed, not Luftwaffe or SS. I knocked at the Colonel's door, an aide opened it, I heard Müller say cheerfully, 'Come in, Padre', and the aide left, leaving us alone. 'I understand you had a successful trip,' he said, pointing to a chair.

'Thank you, yes, very. Thank you for your assistance.'

'Oh, nothing, nothing at all.'

I fidgeted uneasily in my seat. 'The only thing that worries me...'

He interrupted me with a smile. 'Captain von den Velde, no?'

'Yes, he paid me a visit immediately I got back.'

'I imagined he would. But don't worry, Padre. He just tries to throw his weight around. I can handle him. So any time you need some help, don't hesitate to call on me.'

'Except for an army vehicle?'

'Yes, in that respect, I am afraid he was right. In my eagerness to help you, I exceeded my powers. However,' he rose, 'I have now written to Field-Marshal Kesselring, the German commander of Italy, asking him to agree to make Assisi an open city.'

'Fortini, the ex-Mayor, wrote to the Holy See,' I said.

'I know. So maybe if we push from both sides you'll be spared not only bombardments but also visits from the SS.' He shook my hand and accompanied me to the door.

In the afternoon I decided to pay a visit to San Quirico. I had promised to inform my underground headquarters at once about my trip to Abruzzi.

Just as Suora Alfonsina, the slimmest and the prettiest of the sisters, opened the gate for me, I heard a clatter of high heels behind me. A comely young woman with wavy hair swept past me up the staircase, leaving a trace of perfume behind her. 'Franca Covarelli,' the sister said. 'Suora Elena's niece. She is staying at the guest-house.'

'Be sure she doesn't see your charges.'

'How can she? She can't enter the cloister.' The nun opened the side gate for me.

I walked to the oblong building behind the garden, past the oleanders and evergreens and the camouflaged entry to an old underground Roman passage that led out of the cloister. The big room where the men slept at night served as a day room for everybody. People sat on beds, suitcases and wooden boxes. They all rushed towards me. Olga Kropf, who happened to be nearest the door, hugged me to her matronly bosom. 'I'm so glad you're back, Padre!' Giorgio, who had both his arms around his Hella, left her at once. Even Baruch, in his felt slippers, abandoned his primus, where he was cooking something kosher, to come and shake my hand.

'Hello, my children,' I said. Like a magician, I shook my wide sleeves and, lo and behold, several packets of cigarettes fell on the floor. I used to bring them the cigarette rations of the monks, none of whom smoked. But now no one picked up even one packet.

'Mission accomplished, eh?' Giorgio exclaimed. 'Now it's our turn, right?'

'Mission accomplished,' I answered, 'but we have to wait with our next group. Let us sit down.' As they gathered around me, I lit a cigarette and told them about the visit of Captain von den Velde and the need for precautions in view of what he had told me. It would be best, I concluded, to wait a bit and then send someone to Abruzzi to investigate the situation before making our next move.

I saw the bitter disappointment in everybody's face, except that of the tall, bearded man who during my entire report continued to carve the figure of a monk out of a little piece of wood. As I looked at him apologetically, Colonel Paolo Gay raised his pale blue eyes to me. 'I wouldn't have gone anyway,' he said. 'My duty is to stay here and organise the armed resistance.' He looked at his watch and got up. 'Time for the news,' he said. 'From London.'

I knew he was going to Cardelli almost daily to listen to a short-wave radio. 'I'll go with you, Colonel,' I said. I had to talk to Cardelli about placing someone we could trust in Bastia.

At this moment Suora Beata entered the room. 'Doctor,' she addressed Carlo Maionica. 'Sorry to trouble you, but it's urgent.' He instinctively picked up his doctor's bag from a shelf about his bedding. I sensed that this was the first time he was being called by the nuns. Suora Beata looked at me. 'Sister Elena has suddenly been seized with heart pains.'

'I will come along,' I said. I turned to Gay. 'Go ahead, Colonel. I'll join you presently.' I had to stay for I was Sister Elena's father confessor.

The nun led us through a long corridor into the main

building and we entered a small room overlooking the garden. On the bed lay an elderly woman, her eyes shut tight, gasping with pain, her hands clasping her chest. Suora Beata sat by her side and began muttering prayers. Carlo asked her to move away, took Sister Elena's pulse and then checked her blood pressure. He raised her eyelids and examined her eyes, then finally, despite Suora Beata's cry of horror, he bared Sister Elena's chest and put his stethoscope to her heart. Then he raised his head. 'An angina pain,' he said. 'She will be all right if left in peace.'

'We shall pray for her,' Sister Beata said.

The door opened and the Mother Abbess pushed in the young woman I had seen outside a quarter of an hour ago. 'It's against the rules,' she said, 'but you are her closest relative.'

The young girl rushed to the sick nun and took her hand. 'How do you feel, Aunt Elena?'

Maionica was just slipping a nitroglycerine pill into the nun's mouth. 'This ought to help immediately.' He turned to the Mother Abbess. 'Has she had these attacks before?'

'She had rheumatic fever in her youth,' Mother Giuseppina answered.

'That's what I thought. It has resulted in chronic infection of the heart. Her pulse is irregular. You'll have to get her some digitalis from a pharmacy. But there is no immediate cause for alarm.'

'I'll get the medicine right away,' Franca volunteered. 'Please write a prescription. Don't worry, Aunt Elena.' She caressed the woman's cheek. 'Everything will be all right.' She got up, ready to leave, and saw the young man looking helplessly at the Mother Abbess.

'You'd better get another doctor from town; I can't write a prescription, you understand, Mother.'

'*I* don't understand!' Franca said, almost angrily. 'You're a doctor, aren't you?'

Mother Abbess glanced at me. I nodded approval. The nun took Franca's hand. 'My dear child,' she said, 'we all took an oath, but I guess we shall have to include you. Please swear on this holy cross above your aunt's bed that you'll keep secret what I'm about to tell you.'

'I swear. What is it?'

Mother Giuseppina led Franca to the window. 'From the guest-house you can't see the cloistered area, but from here you can.'

Franca opened her mouth and then covered it with her palm. 'There are people there. There are men in the cloister.'

'We are hiding Jews and anti-Fascists in the convent,' Mother Giuseppina said.

Franca turned her face to the young doctor. 'Now I understand, forgive me. Oh, Mother, you can trust me! I worked in the underground in Rome before coming here.' She turned to Carlo once more. 'Anything I can do to help you, please just tell me.'

The doctor nodded. 'First help your aunt. Get another doctor to write a prescription. And don't mention that I was here.'

'I shall give you an address, Franca. I would have called him,' the Mother Abbess said, 'but Suora Elena was in such terrible pain.'

Maionica glanced at the nun, now resting comfortably. He picked up his bag, but as he was about to go through the door he turned and looked at the girl, as if he was seeing her for the first time. Franca raised her head and hid her blush with a smile of thanks. 'One more thing,' Carlo said. 'If you could get this doctor to write a prescription for insulin, I would be grateful.' He turned to me. 'Mrs Weiss has run out of her supply. Diabetes.' Then he looked at the Abbess and she nodded.

Now I was free to approach Sister Elena and offer her my spiritual help. I took her hand. 'You'll be all right,' I said, reassuringly. 'I know. And Doctor Maionica is a good doctor. From Trieste.'

'Thank you, Padre.'

Then I saw Carlo in the doorway. He stood there as if glued to the spot, pretending he was waiting for me, but his eyes were focused on the girl. I looked back and saw Franca, openly, candidly, returning the man's stare. I smiled to myself. Love at first sight, I thought. In the cloister! And then I turned to the sick nun. 'Let's now say together, "Our Father, who are in heaven".'

. . .

I mounted the dark staircase of No. 20 Via San Paolo. On the third floor, I knocked and called out, 'It's me. Padre Rufino.' The door opened and Giovanni Cardelli looked around to make sure that no one else was in sight, then quickly let me in and locked the door behind me. Bent over a map I saw Colonel Gay and his San Quirico companion, an air force lieutenant, Antonio Podda.

'Sit down, Padre,' Gay said. He looked at Cardelli. 'Continue, please.'

'The area most suitable for organising a guerilla unit', Giovanni said, 'would, of course, be Monte Subasio itself. It is covered with dense forest, and should the Nazis attempt to penetrate it the guerillas could either attack them from above or disperse easily. On the other hand, small bands could descend at night and mine the main highway or the railway tracks and cause great damage to the German supply routes to the front line.'

'So let's start,' Gay said impatiently. 'Or the Allies will defeat the Germans without our participation and then we won't have any say in the affairs of Italy after the war.'

'Five divisions are already being raised and armed by the Allies,' Podda corrected. He was a wiry, little man, some fifteen years younger than Gay.

'Who knows when they'll see action? Our job is to organise the resistance behind enemy lines. How many men could you get me, Cardelli?'

'Thirty, perhaps fifty,' answered the town's chief delegate to the National Committee for the Liberation.

'How soon?'

'Give me a few weeks. We must proceed very carefully. I would have to screen every volunteer personally.'

Gay turned to me. 'You, Padre, could help us by reporting on the German troop movements. You could easily observe the traffic from San Damiano. Have you noticed any unusual activity near the front?'

I spread my hands. 'No, it seems that the war has come to a halt for the winter. Except for some patrol activity and skirmishes.'

'It always does,' the Colonel said, professionally. 'But we must prepare for the spring—for the Allied invasion of France and the offensives of both the British Eighth Army and the American Fifth Army in Italy. And we must help them by sabotage and guerilla raids behind the enemy lines.'

Cardelli went to the window and examined the street below. People were scurrying in and out of the shops and buildings; three carabinieri walked slowly towards the Porta San Giacomo; a German officer halted his black Mercedes, aimed his Leica at the ancient Palazzo Locatelli, took a photograph, then drove on.

'Cardelli,' I said, gazing at a huge red banner spread over the road proclaiming 'I'm advancing. Follow me. Mussolini'. 'I had a visit this morning from one Captain von den Velde, the SS and the Gestapo head of the area, with headquarters in Bastia. He seems to know a lot about what's going on in town.' Giovanni turned to me, alarmed. 'I don't mean about our activities. But, for example, he knew that I went to Abruzzi yesterday.'

'Everybody knew that.'

'Well, anyway, you have your men in the Casa del Comune. Could you get someone to work for von den Velde, so we can be forewarned about any razzia in the town?'

'I shall try,' Cardelli said. 'A girl. A pretty girl, who types a little and speaks German. The Captain, I understand, has an eye for pretty girls.'

Suddenly the old walls of the room reverberated with the roar of approaching engines. The two officers rushed to the window. The sky thundered above us and I caught glimpses of silver wings, painted with stars and stripes and 'USAAF' signs flashing by. Almost at once the sirens sounded the alarm. Wardens with red armbands appeared on the streets and chased people into their houses. But they thronged to their windows and balconies, no longer afraid, because the plane formation had already passed over the town. Distant explosions were heard as the bombs reached their targets. 'Long live Italy!' yelled the Colonel at the top of his voice.

'They are attacking my aerodrome!' Lieutenant Podda cried. 'My squadron was based at Sant'Egidio.'

We listened to the whining of dive-bombers, the explosions, the firing of anti-aircraft guns, and then suddenly in the midst of this uproar I heard Podda scream. 'They scored a direct hit! Look! An American plane is hit!' I saw smoke engulfing the tail of the plane. A moment later two white parachutes opened, the one immediately after the other, below the plane, but the anti-aircraft fire continued in that direction. 'They are shooting at the men, the bastards!' Podda exclaimed. Low clouds covered the parachutes just as the plane plummeted into a forest. The other planes, having discharged their loads, now flew back over our heads, the anti-aircraft fire ceased, and then, as abruptly as it had all started, the raid was over. 'They must have shot them down,' Gay sighed.

Cardelli left the window and motioned to the two officers. I saw them push a heavy chest of drawers out of the way, then Cardelli lifted up two planks of wood and with the help of Podda pulled out an army short-wave receiver. They put the radio on the table and Cardelli began to turn the knobs. There was Hungarian music, and German marches, and an Arab newscaster's voice. Finally he halted at the faint signal of the Italian song of resistance. He raised the volume. 'Our station,' he said proudly.

'This is the Voice of CNL—the National Committee for the Liberation,' I heard, 'and here is the news from occupied Italy.' I looked admiringly at Giovanni. 'The Government of the Social Republic of Salo today extended the age of draftees to thirty-five in order to speed up the formation of five Italian divisions promised by the Duce to the Führer.'

'Five divisions on each side,' snorted the Colonel. 'That balances—but it also erases any possibility of our playing a part in the shaping of our own destiny.'

'Shhh!' Cardelli said. 'Listen!'

'All men up to the age of sixty not drafted by the army will be called up to join a labour force to help the Nazi war machine.'

It was now my turn to sigh. It meant more paper work, more printing at night—more exemptions to be made for the Jewish refugees under their Catholic names.

'In the Foligno area,' the speaker continued, 'our heroic partisans have carried out a successful ambush on a German army convoy, blowing up three ammunition trucks and killing three German soldiers. The Nazi commander of the city has promised a large reward for capturing the suspected leader of the partisans, the former Mayor of Foligno, Francesco Innamorati.'

'You see,' Gay exclaimed, 'Foligno is active, but we are not!'

'I'll get you your men soon,' Cardelli said. 'Pazienza, Gay.'

The voice suddenly became inaudible as disturbance interfered with the reception. Cardelli quickly tried to adjust the knobs, but to no avail. 'The Germans! They are jamming the station.' Angrily he turned the radio off. The receiver was again hidden away under the floor.

'We must all work together, gentlemen,' Cardelli said. 'The military and the politicians, the lay leaders and the clergy—all the anti-Fascists. Even though the moment the war is won we'll be at each other's throats again.'

'What do you mean?' Gay asked.

'Well, you, Colonel, are a monarchist; we want a republic after the war, and we, even we, differ between ourselves. Our National Committee for the Liberation is composed of six parties. And everyone wants a different form of republic. We have Catholics, socialists, communists, liberals, etcetera, etcetera, all united at the moment. But none of our six parties wants the monarchy to continue.'

'Why?'

'Because your King, Colonel, has contributed to the disaster we are in. Although he has now declared war against the Germans, he supported Mussolini and in 1940 he declared war on the Allies.'

'We all', the Colonel said, 'have our share of the guilt. Even the Vatican. Its Lateran Pact strengthened Mussolini, its Concordat with Germany helped Hitler. We Italians must now try to redeem ourselves—including the King and the Pope.' Slowly he put on his coat. 'Get me the men, Cardelli,' he said. 'Soon. I need time to train them. I want to go into action by March.'

At the Bishop's Palace another policy meeting was about to begin. In the library were Bishop Nicolini, Don Aldo Brunacci and Father Michele Todde. They constituted a triumvirate in charge of Catholic refugees from the south, of whom as many as two thousand were already in Assisi. But our work was overlapping more and more. Groups of Jewish refugees would come to the Basilica of St Francis and approach the tall, ascetic-looking Franciscan father for help, or they would come to the Laboratorio di San Francesco, where Don Aldo, the canon of the Cathedral of San Rufino, conducted his daily mass. And they, of course, would in turn send the people to me.

When I arrived, Nicolini raised his pudgy little hand in welcome. 'We have been waiting for you, Padre,' he said. 'I have brought some important news from Perugia with me and immediately summoned my council. Sit down, please. But first tell us about your trip.'

I reported my journey in detail, and the Bishop's cherubic face lit up with delight. But when I described von den Velde's unexpected visit and his announcement that the Germans were trying to close the routes over the Sangro, Nicolini's smile instantly faded. 'We have over one hundred people in Perugia,' he said, 'three hundred in Florence and...'

'Three hundred here,' I finished.

'And they have all been looking forward to escaping to the Allied side. Not counting the thousands of others hiding in other cities.'

'In a week, Monsignore,' I said, 'we ought to send someone, perhaps Battaglia, to Abruzzi, to check on the situation. Perhaps von den Velde was just bluffing. Or perhaps the Germans will fail.'

'They didn't fail in the Apennines,' Padre Todde said soberly.

'I had a meeting in Perugia with Cardinal della Costa's emissary, Giorgio La Pira,' the Bishop went on. 'Through him the Cardinal has asked me to absorb more people into our town if we cannot send them through the front line. He feels it's the safest place: because of its holy character, and its many monasteries, and because we have such excellent documents, and finally, because of Colonel Müller.'

'All our monasteries are full up, Monsignore,' I cried in despair.

Don Brunacci rubbed his eyebrows, which were so unusually thick that they should have been either trimmed or combed. 'Then you must do what we are doing, Padre. Place the people in private homes. That is, if the road through to Abruzzi is closed.'

The Bishop sighed. 'Let's hope it is not.'

'Let's hope so,' I said.

There was an urgent knocking at the door and Emilia's face appeared. 'Monsignore,' she said to her uncle, 'there is a little boy here, sent by Padre Sebastiano from the Basilica of Santa Maria degli Angeli. He says it's very urgent and—very private.'

The Bishop heaved his bulky body out of the chair. 'The Pontiff knows how to delegate his duties,' he said. 'I apparently do not. They come to me with every little detail.'

He left, but he was back within a minute. He stormed back into the room, snapping his fingers. 'Padre Rufino, I want you to go immediately to the Basilica with the boy. The two Americans—the two American pilots they shot down have made their way there. You must help them.' The Bishop of Assisi did not know how to delegate his duties? I smiled sadly. He certainly did. He simply passed them on to me. 'I'm certain that the Germans are looking all over for them. Be quick—hide them well and include them in the first transport across the front line.'

I made my obeisance. Outside, an emaciated little blond boy waited for me. He grasped my hand and we started. 'We don't have much time left before the curfew,' I said.

'No, Padre.'

'What's your name?'

'Pio Caianella.'

'Haven't I seen you before? You are one of the Basilica choirboys, aren't you?'

'Yes.'

'How did the Americans find their way there? Who brought them?'

'I did,' the boy answered. 'I searched for them in the forest, trying to get to them before the Germans did. I brought them through the forest and orchards down to the Basilica.'

'In their uniforms?'

'Yes,' the boy smiled. 'It wasn't easy, but I did it.'

Pio Caianella, aged ten or eleven, I thought, ought to be the first man Colonel Gay should enlist in his guerilla unit.

The village of Santa Maria degli Angeli swarmed with German troops. The army vehicles raced through the streets and two planes circled above the forest. The Italians stood on their balconies, watching the show. 'They've found the wreckage,' I heard someone say, 'but they're still searching for the pilots' bodies.'

The 'bodies' were resting comfortably on cots in the Grotto of St Francis below the Rose-Garden Chapel in the back yard of the Basilica. They were wearing monks' habits; their uniforms had been burned in the furnace. Father Sebastian was concerned because one of the men's arms had been grazed by a bullet and he needed medical attention. He also worried that the two would betray themselves if the Nazis or the OVRA came in and lined up all the brothers and asked them questions in Italian.

The American pilots were both very young, very tall and too handsome to be Franciscan brothers. Fortunately their zucchettos covered their crew cuts. A small, bearded seminarist, Emanuele Testa, was brought in as an interpreter. Through him I told the Americans that I represented the Bishop, that the curfew was about to begin and that Germans were all around us, so that they would have to remain where they were and pray, together with the rest of the brothers, that the Nazi soldiers would not think of entering the Basilica. I also said that a doctor would come tomorrow to attend to the man's wound, and that they should not worry because their hiding-place was situated in the garden of thornless roses which had lost their thorns when Brother Francis had thrown himself on them. But they didn't seem to be reassured. Perhaps they weren't Catholics. It was hard to tell by their names. One was called Danny and he was from San Francisco, and freckle-faced Frank talked with a funny drawl, which, he explained was the Southern dialect of the United States. But the moment I told them that we might attempt to smuggle them back to the Allied side the two men burst with joy. They shook my hand, they patted my back, they exclaimed 'Gee, thanks, Father' and 'Grazie, Padre. Molte grazie.'

As I was leaving I thanked the young seminarist for his help. 'Isn't Innamorati of Foligno married to a Testa woman from Assisi?' I asked.

'She's my aunt,' Emanuele Testa said. 'Why?'

'He's a leader of a guerilla unit there, isn't he?'

'He is,' the young man said proudly. 'And my sister Carla is in that unit, too. She carries a gun.'

I shook his hand. 'Guard those Allies of ours well.'

Outside it was almost getting dark and I started to walk fast towards San Damiano. Suddenly I felt a wetness on my face. It is beginning to rain, I thought, and looked up, but it wasn't rain. Soft white flakes of snow were falling from the sky and, as I reached half-way to my monastery, the road, the rooftops, the pine-covered summit of Monte Subasio were all covered by a thin white blanket. The engine noises and the German soldiers' voices subsided. They had probably given up their search—at least for the night. I felt happy, for I thought of the distant days when I, together with my brothers Luigi and Enrico, had gone sliding down the Montenero mountain in Deruta on our primitive, home-made wooden sleighs.

It snowed in Assisi for a whole week. The Germans gave up their search, assuming that the bodies of the American pilots would by now have been covered by the snow. The men stayed at the Basilica of Santa Maria degli Angeli. Frank's wounded arm began to heal with the help of Doctor Maionica, and plans had been made for sending the Americans and a number of people from San Quirico across the front line.

As soon as German bulldozers had cleared the roads of snow, word was sent to Battaglia and he bicycled to Pescocostanzo on a scouting mission. He returned at night and I gave him wine to warm him up. 'What's the news?' I asked eagerly.

He wiped the dirt from his face. 'Bad, I'm afraid, Padre. A German patrol has ambushed your men in the mountains on a smuggling trip. They killed Luigi. Vittorio escaped, but the old man in the mountains, the forester, has been taken by the Gestapo.'

Painfully, I closed my eyes. Luigi, the man of few words, the father of six children, the provider of food for our refugees for the winter, was dead. And old Francesco would no longer sit, peaceful and confident, with his long-stemmed pipe at his fireside in his mountain cabin, and would probably rot in some German concentration camp. And my Jewish refugees and the American pilots would have to stay in hiding. The last escape route out of Nazi-occupied Italy had been closed. They would all have to wait now, until the end of the war.

XIII

I remember that winter of 1944 so well, perhaps because, although the world was engulfed in the most terrible war, there was something so peaceful, so pastoral about our town, covered more often than not by a blanket of snow; and because of the closeness we monks and priests enjoyed with our fellow men who had found refuge in our monasteries. Captain von den Velde did not reappear. And 'our Colonel' as the people of Assisi used to call him, though busy converting schools into hospitals for German soldiers wounded at Anzio and Cassino, and hotels into convalescent centres, always had time to go daily to the Basilica of St Francis, to prostrate himself in front of the crypt of our saint, to attend Padre Todde's mass, to take his afternoon walk, unescorted, around the city, rain or snow, and to see me, quite often for a glass of Moselle or a game of chess.

Two thousand soldiers had been moved into Assisi to recover from wounds, physical and mental, and with the soldiers and the refugees our population of 5,000 was almost doubled. How many among the two thousand Catholic refugees living in private houses were not Catholic was impossible to say. There was now no way out of Italy. So, following the agreement reached by Cardinal della Costa and our Bishop, the Jews under his jurisdiction and those sent to him by other archbishops were to obtain documents from us and, if they wished, were to settle in Assisi. While Cardelli and his men were recruiting partisans for Colonel Gay, I and my brothers were going from house to house to ask the civilians, who already had Catholic refugees lodged with them, to take in more. Of course our people had good documents, but how often did the prospective landlords, after seeing the oriental features and the eyes which bore the imprint of three thousand years of suffering, smile benevolently, nod their approval and take in the new lodgers, without pay!

Every few days I would wrap myself up warmly against the cold wind blowing from the mountains, and visit the French, the Spanish, the American and the German sisters, the convents of the Stigmata, of Jesus the Child and of the Missionaries of Santa Maria and many others, and when weather permitted and a Volkswagen was provided by Colonel Müller, I would visit the Abbeys of Vallingeno and San Benedetto, the Hermitage, Montefalco, Gubbio, Spello. All the monasteries and churches in Assisi and the surrounding countryside were filled with Jews disguised as monks or nuns, or hiding behind the double grilles of the Enclosure, or living with false papers in the pilgrims' guest-houses attached to these houses.

One particular day, I followed my usual itinerary in town, stopping at the Colettines for a concert. I sat with Albert and Maria Finzi of Antwerp, and other Jewish refugees who filled the choir's benches to listen to a chorus of white-clad nuns singing Gregorian chants to the accompaniment of the organ, beautifully played by Albert Fano, the white-haired seventy-year-old Jewish professor from Milan Conservatory. At about four o'clock I halted for a brief visit two hundred metres further on, at the Benedictine monastery where a dozen of my charges were boarded, and then crossed the street to San Quirico.

Our Headquarters was about to close for the day. Giorgio Kropf as usual sat at his battered typewriter, Nino Maionica had a pad and a seal in front of him, and Pali Jozsa was forging the signatures of dead or imprisoned German commanders from the south. New documents, identity cards, releases from the army, labour permits—documents for those whose photographs were carried to Assisi by Gino Battaglia or Giorgio La Pira—all had to be ready for Luigi Brizi, who slept all day and printed all night, with the help of his son, who attended to the shop during the day and rested God knows when.

Gruel was cooking on the primus, attended by Baruch in his slippers and skull-cap. The women sat around, darning their menfolk's socks or knitting shawls. Amazingly, I had discovered a few days earlier, they were knitting shawls for Colonel Gay's Italian partisans who were still enjoying the warmth of their houses, awaiting the call of Cardelli. And then Colonel Gay himself came in. With a smile, he took me by the arm and led me proudly to his greatest artistic creation. He led me across the cold courtyard, its oleanders covered by snow, across the old cemetery with stones inscribed 'The Lord gave rest', and flung open the cracked wooden door of a shed where, lo and behold, the broken old lavatory seat was gone and in its place there was a wooden throne, fit for a king, finely carved with decorations and cherubs and angels. Ruefully, he spread his arms. 'Pazienza, Padre,' he said. 'That's all I can do while waiting to do greater things for my country.'

When we returned, I visited the other room. A few of the young couples were holding hands. I saw Carlo Maionica with Franca Covarelli; they were now engaged. Whether it was out of her devotion to the newly found cause or her love for the handsome young doctor did not matter; Franca was one of the best members of the underground. She stole special forms from the Casa del Comune, she visited tobacconists to buy state stamps for our documents, never too many at a time, and she spent hours at the post office, finding southern names and addresses. She helped me to build up a vast spy network of porters, clerks and charwomen who were working for the Nazis and the OVRA. Cardelli may have provided the young, attractive German-speaking woman, but it was Franca who secured her employment with von den Velde.

At the headquarters, work finished and the men now joined us. Giorgio joined Hella, and Pali joined Deborah, who had stopped painting her latest portrait of St Francis talking to the birds. I was about to leave when Carlo told me that although Franca's aunt Elena had recovered completely, Mrs Weiss, the diabetic, was in bed and badly needed insulin. Did I know of a reliable doctor who could write a prescription? The one whom Mother Giuseppina recommended had started to become very suspicious and refused to write any more. I knew of one—Dr Paci, who already was on Cardelli's list. The insulin would be in tomorrow morning, I told Maionica.

Outside, snow had begun to fall. The people fell silent. The dark grey of the late winter afternoon began shrouding the rooms. Then, softly, Hanna Gelb began to sing. She sang in

Hebrew but her words were translated for me. It was 'Yam Kinneret', the song of the 'Sea of Galilee', the lake in Palestine that was sacred to them and sacred to us. And the others joined her, singing sweetly in the strange language which they did not know except through the words of prayers and songs. And I, Padre Rufino, sang with them. It was a haunting, sad, beautiful melody that expressed the longing of the people for the land from which they had been expelled two thousand years earlier, and it was sung on a cold white winter afternoon in a Nazi garrisoned Italian town.

Abruptly, the side door opened and Sister Amata burst in. 'Oh, Padre Guardiano,' she said. 'Mother Abbess learned you were here. She wants to see you.'

Dutifully, I followed the familiar route to the parlour. I saw the emaciated face of Mother Giuseppina behind the window, her hands folded. 'Padre Rufino,' she said, 'I have something to tell you. I know that you are on your way down to the Basilica of Santa Maria degli Angeli, to visit your Jews and Americans.' I watched her close her eyes and swallow hard before going on. 'I have just heard on the radio that the Germans have ambushed a group of guerilla leaders in Foligno. They shot without trial the former Mayor Innamorati, the priests Merlini and Merli, and a girl, Carla Testa, from Assisi. Her brother, Emanuèle Testa...'

I sighed in deep despair. 'I know, Mother, I know...I will tell him.'

'Thank you, Padre,' the Mother Abbess said. 'Bless you.'

'Bless you, Mother. And pray for them today.'

I started on my way down to the Basilica, painfully rehearsing my message to Emanuele Testa. I will never forget the date, and in the history of the Italian resistance, it will not be forgotten either: 24 January 1944.

The snow melted and in the middle of February the rains came. It was pouring outside, the rain drumming on my roof, when I was awakened shortly before dawn by Giorgio Kropf, who asked me to rush to San Quirico. He had braved the curfew and the weather to come over to San Damiano to tell me that during the night Signora Clara Weiss had died. The insulin supplied by Dr Paci had not helped. The Nazis did not get her, but the disease had claimed its victim, the first Jew to die in Assisi.

The two of us rushed back to San Quirico along the muddy road. The rain kept away the German patrols and we reached the convent safely. I was ushered into the room where once Suora Elena had lain ill and where Signora Weiss alias Bianchi now lay dead.

Don Aldo Brunacci was there, because he was in charge of Catholic refugees and it was obvious that if Mrs Weiss were to be buried she could not be buried as a Jew. Don Aldo and I exchanged glances and we both opened our arms with a gesture which said, 'Well, what can you do, death is part of life.' And we both sighed because we were already having to think of what to do next. Brunacci spoke first. 'Padre Rufino,' he said, 'I shall order a coffin and will offer prayers to our Lord Jesus and place a cross over her grave.' Then he glanced uneasily at Olga Cantoni, Mrs Weiss's best friend, sitting in a chair and lamenting. 'There is no other way, Signora, you understand?'

'No, no other way,' I added my support. 'For the security of us all. You can of course say your prayers here, in private, before the funeral procession departs from San Quirico.' Signora Cantoni sighed and nodded her approval.

The wooden coffin was ready in the afternoon as the coffin maker happened to have a suitable one. He and the cemetery superintendent were given Dr Paci's certificate attesting to the fact that Signora Clara Bianchi, the Catholic refugee from Foggia, had died of diabetes. And then we all gathered—all the refugees of San Quirico and the nuns and Don Aldo and I. The Jews, ten righteous men, donned their skull-caps and said their prayers—and old Baruch intoned Kaddish, the prayer for the dead and for the living that remain behind. We listened and silently prayed to Jesus Christ for Mrs Weiss, just in case. After all, He was Jewish, too.

And then the coffin was closed, its cover was nailed down and four young men carried it to the two-horse carriage waiting outside. The horses wore blinkers, so that they would walk straight and with dignity, and the harness and the carriage were appropriately dressed in black. And we followed, with our black umbrellas, through the murky, rainy, winding streets of Assisi, to the cemetery lying just outside the Porta di San Giacomo.

The carriage stopped outside the cemetery, and then our young men carried the coffin over the gravel road, through the wide gate, past the magnificent mausoleums of the old families of Assisi—the Fiumis, the Tibaldis, the Nepis—to the far end where poorer people were buried in the simple splendour of death under the crosses with their biblical quotations. Their life histories were given simply: dates of birth and death separated by a dash. That dash was their life.

The rain continued to fall, obscuring the houses and the hills around us, pattering on the tombs and the umbrellas and driving against our faces, as Don Aldo read from the Book the appropriate verses of the New Testament and then delivered a eulogy, praising the life of Signora Bianchi who, throughout her seventy years in Foggia, had never forgotten the poor and the needy, never missed a Sunday mass and who would find as good a welcome in the Umbrian land as if it were her own land of Puglia. I looked around; most of the people I knew—the externs of San Quirico, the Jews of San Quirico, a few priests and curious bystanders—but among them I noticed a man who looked familiar, and yet I could not see his face. Dark sunglasses shielded his eyes. I sighed. Even here at a funeral ceremony an OVRA man had to be present. None of us had ever managed to get away from him. Only Mrs Weiss.

As we left the cemetery, the rain settled into a gentle drizzle. I took a short cut back to my monastery, going towards the Porta di San Pietro, but as I was passing the Piazza di San Francesco, I suddenly decided to go and see Colonel Müller. I had not seen him for more than two weeks, and he was still the best source of information on what was happening in the town and what might lie in store for us.

Signor Rossi was in the lobby and he clasped his hands together when he saw me. 'Nostro colonnello sta malato,' he announced. 'He has the flu and he's resting in his suite.'

'When a person has flu, I am sure he needs spiritual help.' And I crossed the lobby.

The hotel owner dashed after me, led me to a door on the second floor and disappeared before I was able to knock. 'Herein, bitte!' I pushed the door open and saw Müller sitting on a chair, wrapped in a flannel dressing-gown, a towel around his neck, his bare feet immersed in a bowl of steaming water. He was sniffing at an inhaler. 'Oh, Padre, come in.'

What Signor Rossi had called a suite was simply the best and largest room in the hotel, with a balcony overlooking the main highway and the village of Santa Maria degli Angeli. It was furnished with a bed, a sofa, an armchair, a desk and a few chairs. Framed photographs of the Colonel's wife and children, as well as those of an elderly couple and a grey-haired man in a black cassock, stood on the desk. On the wall above the sofa hung a painting of a town square with a fountain and a Gothic church with a Gothic sign beneath it: 'Eichstätt'. The painting was flanked by two diplomas—one was a university degree, the other indicated membership of the Medical Association. No war citations, of which the Colonel must have had quite a number, were exhibited in the room. But to my amazement, over his bed, I noticed a familiar Italian diploma. It attested to the fact that on 7 February 1944 Colonel Valentin Müller had become a member of our International Society for Franciscan Studies. Chapeau bas, as they say in French. I take my hat off to you, Arnaldo Fortini.

The Colonel indicated an armchair. 'I'm so glad you came. It's funny to see a sick doctor, isn't it? But we have a remedy. Kindly open my desk, the bottom drawer on your right.' I did as ordered. 'Now fetch the bottle.' I returned with a bottle labelled 'Cognac Medicinal'. 'Now give me two glasses, please.'

Humorously, I protested. '*I* don't have the flu.'

Colonel Müller lifted the glasses towards the window to make sure that the level of the golden liquid in them was even. 'Preventive medicine,' he said and handed me a drink. 'Cin cin!'

'Salut!' I answered in French. One learns a few foreign words here and there. A modest sip warmed me up right away; there is a lot to be said for preventive medicine.

'Problems or a social visit?' Müller asked.

'Social, purely social. No answer from Field-Marshal Kesselring about proclaiming Assisi an open city?'

'No, not yet.' The Colonel smiled. 'But meanwhile we are a hospital and convalescent town—thanks to Avvocato Fortini.'

'Which means curfews, SS patrols and perhaps even razzias.'

'I will write to Kesselring again. Maybe my request got lost in the mail.'

'Still, as long as you stay here, Colonello, I'm sure everything will be all right. As a matter of fact I haven't seen Captain von den Velde since the day I met him.'

'No wonder. He has been on home leave. Everyone gets leave once in a few years, everyone but me. But don't worry, Padre. You have my telephone number?'

'Yes, of course.' Not only did I have it. The number, 210, had become public knowledge and the people of the town would call the Colonel in any emergency such as the requisitioning of Francesco Pettirosi's taxi or Pio Caianella's bicycle. And our Commandante della Piazza was never too busy to call his military police and order them to return whatever the Germans had taken.

Time and again my eyes wandered to the silver-framed photograph of the priest on the desk and the Colonel finally caught my look. 'My uncle,' he explained. 'I almost became a priest myself. I even attended a seminary, but my parents decided that one in the family was enough. So instead of healing souls I heal bodies. Have a bit more medicine.'

We had another drink, which mellowed me completely. 'I hope, Colonello,' I said, 'that after the war you'll come back for a visit and bring your family along.'

'Oh, absolutely,' he said.

'The news from the Russian front is not the best, is it?' I said in a commiserating tone.

'No, I'm afraid not.' He sighed. He was a good man, the Colonel, but he was a patriot and naturally he wanted his country to win the war. I never dared to discuss Hitler and Nazism with him, but I never heard him say anything good about them either, nor saw him raise his arm in a 'Heil Hitler' salute as all other Germans and even many Italians did.

'I hope you'll get over the flu quickly, Colonello.' I rose and blessed him with the sign of the cross.

'Thank you, Padre. And come again. Any time. Forgive me...' He pointed at his bare feet submerged in the water.

'Of course, of course.' As I was closing the door behind me, I caught a glimpse of him picking up his inhaler again.

Passing the reception desk, I indicated to Signor Rossi in Italian sign language that the Colonel would soon be back on his feet, and walked out into the Via Frate Elia. It was now getting dark, and the mist was clinging to the cobblestones and ancient walls. A military Volkswagen stood under the yellow light of a street lamp, and I saw an officer alighting from it. He waved to me. 'Buona sera, Padre.' It was Captain von den Velde, back from his leave.

I waited for him and we shook hands. 'You had a nice, long rest?' I inquired politely.

'Too long, I'm afraid.' He gestured towards the town. 'I am responsible for the security of two thousand soldiers here. I understand our Stadtkommissar is ill. I have come to cheer him up.'

He saluted. I started down the street. After a while I glanced back over my shoulder. The SS captain was still standing outside the hotel, his dark silhouette almost immobile, his face turned towards me. My heart began to beat faster as I quickened my step, not daring to look back.

XIV

One afternoon I was at San Quirico, listening to Baruch and his son-in-law explaining their big problem to me. Soon it would be spring, and then Passover, and for the Jewish Easter kosher was not enough. It had to be especially kosher. No bread, no flour, new plates and a cauldron in which they could boil their utensils. I could hardly concentrate on the exposition of their dietary laws, and my eyes kept darting to my watch. It was now half-past four.

In the morning a few of our young men had gone to Perugia, carrying identity cards and draft releases in their shoes, ready for delivery to the refugees. They had done it before, and I myself and other monks and priests had done it. We went either by train or in one of Geremia del Bianco's taxis, but Don Brunacci usually bicycled. Our destination was always the same, the headquarters at the church of San Andrea in the parish of Porta di Santa Susanna, on the Via della Sposa. Jews had come and gone there, but there were always at least a hundred of them in the town, some in the church's outhouses, some in private homes, and *their* Father Guardian was Federico Don Vincenti, a small, thin, white-haired man of sixty, of peasant stock like me. My superior was Bishop Nicolini, his was the Archbishop of Perugia, Mario Vianello. But although the Jews seemed safe in Perugia, we still had to provide them with documents. They were not blessed with a Brizi.

The day was beautiful, and so warm that everyone felt spring was coming. The past few months had been peaceful. On that particular day not only Giorgio Kropf went to Perugia, as he had often done before, but also Pali Jozsa and Bruno Fano, Professor Fano's son, a musician in his own right, who also stayed at the Convent of St Colette. And at the last moment they were joined by Colonel Gay and Lieutenant Podda, who were about to leave the cloister to lead the two dozen men Cardelli had provided and who were already waiting for them in the mountains. Everyone had promised to return by the one o'clock train. They were already three and a half hours late.

I looked around me and I could sense the atmosphere getting heavier by the minute. The sun was setting; there should have been another train half an hour ago. Giorgio's father, Giulio Kropf, was talking to his wife, reassuring her, but from the nervous twitch of his little eyes behind his glasses I could sense that he was terribly worried.

The fiancées of Giorgio and Pali took it in turns to peer through a crevice on to the street. It was almost five when Hella suddenly yelled, 'Colonel Gay! I see Colonel Gay! . . . Alone!' She ran frantically towards the garden gate leading to the courtyard. I rushed to join her, and the others followed me. The outside bell rang sharply, we heard the main gate open and close, then the key turned in our gate and Suora Beata ushered a tired, sweating Paolo Gay inside.

'They were caught!' he gasped. 'The OVRA men have taken them to the Perugia Gestapo headquarters. I managed to escape.'

Deborah, Jozsa's fiancée, burst out sobbing. Hella bit her lip and threw her arms around her sister. Giorgio Kropf's mother buried her head in her husband's chest, weeping, 'Oh, God, my God!' The others began nervously plying Gay with questions, terrified that the men would reveal that Jews were hiding here.

At last, I thought with despair, the enemy has caught up with us. The honeymoon with Colonel Müller was over, the more powerful forces had won. But I tried to compose myself, and reassure them. 'Please, please don't get panicky, my children! We must keep calm. Send someone to fetch a glass of water for Colonel Gay. Now, Paolo, tell us what happened.'

He told us. Sitting on his bed in the big room of the outhouse, surrounded by everybody who was hiding in San Quirico, he described how they had arrived safely at the church, delivered the documents to Don Vincenti, and then, because the weather was warm and there was plenty of time before their return train, they had taken a walk through the Via dei Priori. They went past the beautiful fountain in the Piazza IV November, then, when they reached the medieval Palace of the Captain of the People, they decided to have a meal and entered a trattoria. Gay went straight to the men's room. As he was leaving it, he heard an Italian sitting at an adjacent table bend over to Jozsa asking him what time it was. 'Eleven thirty,' Pali answered and suddenly the man got up, whipped out his OVRA card and a pistol and said, 'You are under arrest, all of you!' Then he turned to his companions, obviously also OVRA men. 'This may be that Slav who killed the priest in Foligno.'

'You have heard about the priest who collaborated with the Germans,' Paolo Gay explained, 'and who was executed two days ago by Yugoslav partisans?' I nodded, and the Colonel went on with his story.

All the OVRA men drew their guns. 'Let's take them to Gestapo headquarters,' their leader said. There was an uproar in the restaurant and people rushed to leave their tables. Gay quickly retreated into the men's room and came out only when the restaurant was practically empty.

The Colonel asked for a cigarette and I pulled one from my pocket. The women kept crying. 'What shall we do now?'

Franca Covarelli asked soberly. She reminded me that we also had to think of the others. 'We'd better warn everyone, at least those in the convents,' she said. 'If they break down under questioning...' Delicately, she did not use the word 'torture', but I knew what she meant.

'They won't break down,' I managed to say firmly, but I was aware of the quaver in my voice. I looked at the window. The sunset was giving way to dusk. 'I'll see Colonel Müller right away. Franca, you go the Basilica of Santa Maria degli Angeli and alert Father Sebastian. Can you manage to return before the curfew?' She nodded. 'And just in case, we have to warn all the monasteries.' Immediately two Maionica brothers and Colonel Gay volunteered to go. 'Carlo and Nino will manage,' I said. 'You'd better stay here, Paolo. If they come while I am gone, and let's hope they won't, get everyone out fast through the Roman passage into the fields.'

The officer of the Italian Army's General Staff saluted with faint humour. 'Right!'

Suddenly we heard bells ringing in the distance. My throat tightened with fear. The others froze. I saw their lips counting, 'Four...five...six...' Franca smiled. 'It's for vespers. And I think it's from San Pietro.' The other bells of the town chimed in. It was such a lovely, peaceful melody, sounding more beautiful to me at this moment than any Gregorian chant, even played by Professor Fano. We all breathed a sigh of relief, for after the Nazi round-up we had devised a warning system. The local patrolling was done by carabinieri and German troops stationed at the Via Fontenbella, next to the Hotel Giotto; but truckloads of Gestapo and SS troops driving from the direction of Bastia and turning up the road to Assisi, right opposite the Basilica of Santa Maria degli Angeli, meant a razzia, especially if they came at night. There was always someone on the look-out in the Basilica's belfry, ready to ring the bells—five short peals, then a pause, then five peals again.

I told the Maionica brothers which convents to go to, instructing Franca to impress upon Father Sebastian to be especially on the alert from now on, and finally I asked Paolo Gay to inform the Mother Abbess of the situation.

People were already leaving the churches, in groups silhouetted in the growing dusk of early winter, when I reached the Hotel Subasio and made straight for Colonel Müller's office. I knocked at his door, heard the 'Jawohl?' and when I entered, saw his face buried in a pile of papers on his desk. Then he lifted it and, seeing me, switched to Italian: 'Buona sera, Padre. I don't expect this to be a social visit so late. Am I right? I can read trouble all over your face. Sit down, please.'

I told him what the trouble was. That four young Christian refugees had been arrested in Perugia. 'I see,' I heard the Colonel say, pensively looking through the window. 'The problem is, Padre, that I don't have any control over Perugia. I could have helped you had they been arrested in Assisi, but I can't interfere with...' I drew a deep breath and my disappointment must have communicated itself to Müller. He picked up the phone. 'Bastia! Hauptsturmführer von den Velde, bitte.'

'Oh, no!' I blurted out.

'I want to inquire what it is about. He could call his colleague at Perugia and find out what the men are accused of.'

'Please don't, Colonel.' He put the receiver down before the connection was made. 'I hoped that you could intervene personally, Colonel Müller.'

Müller rubbed his face, hesitantly, but then he lifted the phone again and asked the operator to get him the Gestapo headquarters in Perugia. He waited. I caught myself nervously knotting and unknotting the cord of my habit and clasped my hands together. 'Was? Morgen früh? Danke.' He put the receiver down. 'The connection with Perugia is broken. Your partisans have cut the lines.' I shook my head in anger. My God, Gay's people had started their work without waiting for their leader. And what had they done? Harmed *us*, not the Germans! 'The line is being repaired. I'll call in the morning.'

'Thank you, Colonel. I will come back tomorrow. I'd better get home before curfew.'

I was already at the door when his voice stopped me. 'Padre Rufino! I can only try to help if the men haven't committed any criminal offence, you understand?'

'I'm sure they haven't. I know every one of them personally.'

'Good.'

'Good-night.'

There was no time to see the Bishop. I could not afford to be stopped that night. But on my way back, I entered a public telephone booth, put a token in and dialled. Nicolini himself answered. I informed him that four refugees from the south, Giorgio Cianura, Paolo Macri, Bruno Facco and Antonio Podda, had been arrested in Perugia. There was a moment of stunned silence, then Nicolini's voice sounded again. 'I'll call Avvocato Fortini right away and let him take charge of their case. Of course he won't be able to do anything before tomorrow morning.'

I complimented the Bishop on his excellent idea. Fortini was not only a good, respected Fascist lawyer, but he had also just won national fame for his defence of one of six men accused by the Fascist government of treason in the Verona trial. Ex-Foreign Minister Ciano, Marshal de Bono and three others were executed. Only Tulio Cianetti, the former Minister of Corporations, the man whom Fortini had defended, escaped with a thirty-year sentence. 'Thank you, Monsignore,' I said.

Respectfully I waited for him to hang up, but after a brief pause he spoke again. 'Padre, I would see Sister Clara tonight if I were you. She is not well.'

'Sister Clara?' Then I got the message. One had to be careful on the phone. Nicolini did not refer to the Basilica of Santa Clara, because neither there nor at the Basilica of St Francis did we hide any Jewish refugees. These two holy shrines with the tombs of our saints were not used for fear that, if the Nazis discovered them, they would blow up the basilicas. The Bishop obviously meant the Poor Clares of San Quirico. And by saying 'She is not well' he was alluding to the night of the razzia when I lied, we both lied, by saying that a nun at San Quirico was dying. 'That's what I had planned to do, Monsignore.'

'Good. Bless you.'

I rushed back as fast as I could, but stopped for a moment at the Convent of St Colette. I had to bring the news of his son's arrest to Fano. To my surprise he took it calmly. There was, in this gaunt, white-haired man such an unshakeable pride in being Italian and a descendant of a close supporter of Mazzini that he refused even to change his name. And now he was confident—the only man who knew about the arrests and remained confident—that there was no cause for alarm and that his son had probably by now been released.

How fortunate, I thought, that the young Fano did not share his father's pride and *had* changed his name. I passed my warning on to the petite Mère Hélène, the Mother Superior of the Colettines, and then hurried on to San Quirico.

The Maionica brothers and Franca had already returned, and so we settled down to a long night of waiting. Hardly anyone ate their meal; there was very little of the usual conversation. Even my jokes did not help. Baruch and Gelb put on prayer shawls, rounded up eight more men, and began to pray. The three small Provenzal children cried—quietly sensing the atmosphere of suppressed fear. Only sixteen-year-old Hanna, the youngest of the Gelb sisters, was calm, busily writing up her diary. Next to me I saw Paolo Gay opening his suitcase. He showed me two envelopes.

'My documents,' he said. 'The forged ones and the real ones. The moment the Germans come, the envelope with my real papers goes down the lavatory.'

I turned my head. The Kropfs sat together, staring at the floor. The distant sound of the nuns' singing was just audible. It was long after any canonical hour. The Mother Abbess must have gathered the sisters into the choir room. She didn't have to tell them for whom to pray that day. The Poor Clares were praying for us.

Then the far-away Latin and the near-by Hebrew prayers ceased. The nuns returned to their cells and the Jewish women went to their room, kissing their men good-night and blowing out the candle. In the pale light of the moon, I could see the silhouettes of the men on their beds, fully dressed, their eyes open.

I lay on the empty cot of Nino Podda, in my habit and zucchetto and with my shoes still on. I could hear the restless stirrings of the men, and the sighs of the women from the adjacent room. At the slightest sound from outside—a sudden gust of gathering wind, the stamping of the boots of the patrolling soldiers, the distant barking of dogs—I would start up in fright. Then, as the noises of the evening faded away, I put an arm under my head and remained wakeful, my eyes focused on the ceiling, unblinking. In the silent night I was listening for the sound of bells that were not supposed to ring until the early hours of the morning.

They were not taken to the Gestapo. Signor Mariani, the OVRA man who made the arrest, was a plump, blond and blue-eyed Italian who prided himself on looking Teutonic and whose ambition was to become district head of the OVRA. The road to that appointment led, however, not through the Germans but through the Fascist Prefect and Chief of Police, Armando Rocchi, who surpassed even the Gestapo when he chose to question and torture prisoners himself. Mariani decided that the case warranted Rocchi's personal attention.

As the men neared the restaurant's door, out of reach of Paolo Gay's hearing, Giorgio whispered to Podda. 'Jump out of the window. You're Christian. Even if they catch you, there is not much danger.'

'No,' said Nino Podda. 'I came with you and I stay with you.'

In the street, Mariani opened his leather jacket and whipped out another pistol. People gathered all along the street at a safe distance. Mariani loved to impress the town with his importance, and holding German Lügers in both hands he motioned to his men to escort those arrested and ordered: 'Take them to the Questura.' As soon as they reached the dark three-storeyed building, with its barred windows, he ordered a policeman downstairs to call Armando Rocchi.

A few moments later, the Prefetto himself walked into the windowless, bare-walled room, where a sleepy clerk sat at a typewriter and a lamp shone brightly on a big mahogany desk. The room was adjacent to the cell where the men were being held. Rocchi was a tall, broad man with dark eyes and bushy brows and a few black hairs stretching over his bald head. A bullet scar on his left cheek gave his face a sinister appearance. The clerk sprang to attention. 'Sit down,' Rocchi said, both to the man and to Mariani. The clerk sat down, wide awake now, and he began to listen. He was *our* man in the police headquarters!

'I have four men here,' Mariani pointed. 'One of them

speaks with a Slav accent. For the past few days I have been asking any foreign-looking men I see the same question, "What time is it?" When this fellow answered, I had no doubt he was the person we were looking for.'

'How do you know?' Rocchi asked.

'Instinct,' Mariani said with a smile. 'Police must have instinct. Anyway, I thought if it's the one who killed the Fascist priest in Foligno, we may be on the track of the entire partisan gang.'

'And the others? Do they all have an accent?' Rocchi asked. He opened a silver cigarette-case containing cigarettes and offered one to Mariani in gratitude.

'No, Eccellenza. But they may be the Slav's Italian collaborators. I have no doubt you'll soon find out who they are. The first thing is to check if their documents are forged.'

'Of course,' Rocchi said. He lit the cigarette, then turned the desk lamp around, momentarily blinding Mariani. The OVRA man got up. The light was directed at those to be questioned. Then Rocchi opened his drawer and picked up a thick notebook. He glanced at the police diary on his desk, found the last entry number, and he wrote on the top of his notebook '26 February 1944. No. 308.' Mariani dutifully put in front of him all the documents he had confiscated. 'Send me that Slav first,' Rocchi demanded.

Mariani opened the door. 'Macri Paolo!' he called.

Pali Jozsa entered the room. He jumped at the sound of the door closing behind him, separating him from the others. 'Sit down,' he heard. There was only one chair and the moment he lowered himself into it he felt blinded by the light. Involuntarily, he closed his eyes. 'Your name,' he heard. 'Are you Italian?'

There was no point in lying. The moment his interrogator heard him talk, he would know. 'No,' he said. 'I'm a Yugoslav citizen.' He went on lamely, 'But my mother was German.'

Rocchi smiled shrewdly. 'So you obviously speak German?'

'Natürlich. Da meine Mutter eine Deutsche ist...'

'All right, all right!' Rocchi interrupted in Italian. He didn't know any German except for two words 'Heil Hitler', which he used all day long, even with his Italian colleagues. 'And now... What is your real name?'

'You have my identity card in front of you.'

'Comune di Assisi. Carta d'Identita No. 221,' Rocchi read, Signor Macri Paolo.' He turned to the clerk. 'Why aren't you taking all this down?'

'Oh, yes, of course...' The typewriter started to click fast and the Prefect waited impatiently for the man to catch up. Then he opened Pali's identity card. 'It says here that you were born in Palmi on 19 April 1915. Is that true?'

'Yes.'

'I know the date is true,' Rocchi barked and directed the light straight on to Pali's face. 'I mean, were you born in Italy?' Jozsa said nothing in response. 'All right. You don't have to answer. It's obvious you were not. It's also obvious that your documents are false. Where did you get them?' Again silence. Rocchi leaned forward. Mariani approached the desk, hovering over Pali, waiting for his superior's congratulations. 'Did you kill the priest in Foligno on the night of 22 February, because you and your comrades did not approve of him praising the Italo-German alliance?'

'I was not in Foligno that night or any other night. I have never been to Foligno.'

While the typewriter clicked again, Rocchi made a few notes, then folded his hands in front of him. 'You can prove your innocence by telling me where you were on the night of 22 February.'

'In Assisi.'

'Where in Assisi?'

Pali again became tongue-tied. From his desk Rocchi picked up *La Riscossa* and turned it around, pointing to a notice about two men from Montefalco found guilty by the military tribunal of Perugia of avoiding the army call-up and sentenced to death. They were executed on the spot. 'That's how we deal with those committing the slightest offence against the State. Now, I'll repeat my question. Where were you on the night of 22 February?' There was no answer and Rocchi added, 'I imagine you're a Christian, are you?'

'Yes.'

'Catholic?'

'Yes.'

'Call the prison priest, Signor Mariani, please.'

Jozsa's entire body broke out in sweat. 'I don't understand. I don't need a priest. What for?'

'You need him. We are human. We allow a condemned man to confess and seek spiritual solace before he is put against the wall.'

Pali jumped from his chair. 'You can't execute me without a trial! Those men—they faced the tribunal...'

Rocchi burst out laughing. 'Did you hear that, Mariani?' And the future leader of the OVRA joined in the laughter. 'Fetch Don Giovanni,' Rocchi ordered.

'Right away,' Mariani said. Pali's legs went limp and his face went white. There seemed to be no way out. He could either provide an alibi or be shot, it was as simple as that. And there was really no danger to the others. Just as in the last razzia, the Germans and the OVRA men would come, inquire, but would never dare to break into the nuns' Enclosure. The sisters would certainly verify that Jozsa had stayed at the guest-house, like many other Catholic refugees. Still he said nothing, letting Mariani leave the room, letting Rocchi dictate to the clerk that the accused had failed to provide an alibi and that therefore he, the Prefect, under the emergency powers granted to him due to war, had ordered his execution.

'You may go now,' Rocchi said. 'The priest will come to your cell. Next!' And as Pali opened the door, Rocchi shouted, 'Podda Antonio!'

Nino Podda entered the room and sat in the glare of the light. 'Comune di Assisi. Carta d'Identita No. 363,' Rocchi read. 'So you are all residents of Assisi?' He picked up the phone. 'Give me Assisi,' he said. 'The OVRA headquarters. What? Per Bacco! You bastards', he turned to Podda, 'cut the telephone lines between Perugia and Assisi! Give me Bastia, then. The Gestapo headquarters. Bastia? Captains von den Velde, please! Captain? Heil Hitler! This is Armando Rocchi. We have arrested four young men from your district, one a Slav. Yes—that's right. He might be the man responsible. No, Captain, there is no need for that. We have the same facilities as you to obtain their confession. You are welcome to join me in the investigation. In an hour? Good, thank you. I'm glad to be of service to the Third Reich.'

...

I awoke in a panic. The bells were ringing in the distance. I must have lapsed into a doze. I glanced at the window. It wasn't dawn, it was still night time. Then the bells stopped. I sat on my bed and looked around. The men were sitting in the same position as I; most of them had not slept at all. I had missed the count, but they had not. 'It rang five times,' Otto Maionica said. Then he added quietly, 'Per chi suona la campana...?' For Whom the Bell tolls'—and we all knew the answer as the distant chimes started again and the women rushed into our room. No one had to count again. We knew the bell was tolling for us.

'Come on!' I said, taking immediate charge. 'Without delay!' Everyone was dressed and grabbed his belongings. The women kept filing into our room, as the only way to the garden led through it. 'Follow me!' Paolo Gay said loudly. 'We have seven or eight minutes before they get here.'

It had all been rehearsed before. And as Gay and the young Maionicas pushed the heavy stones away from the camouflaged entry into the tunnel, people at once started to descend into a long underground passage that would lead them a few hundred metres away beyond the city wall near the Porta Moiano. All the extern nuns now began rapidly stripping the beds of linen, pillows and blankets. Everything that had been left behind, even a piece of paper or a handkerchief, was gathered into the straw baskets. In the basement the nuns threw the dirty linen into the cauldrons and piled the blankets and pillows on to the shelves. As I listened to the heavy throb of truck motors shatter the silence of the night, getting closer by the second, all the beds in the two rooms had been stripped and almost everyone was gone.

Outside, two vehicles skidded to an abrupt halt. The quiet street reverberated as the Germans shouted their orders and the soldiers jumped down on to the pavement. The bell clanged urgently and a rifle butt thumped at the iron gate. Both Paolo and I hastily pushed the few remaining stragglers into the tunnel. The nuns deliberately let another minute pass before Suora Amata went to the door. Finally only Paolo, Franca and I were left in the garden. The girl was to remain behind—she was a Catholic refugee legitimately staying at the convent's guesthouse. 'Get in, Paolo, quick!' I said, anxiously eyeing the door of the outhouse. Where were those two damned nuns who were supposed to help Franca cover our exit?

'No, you first, Padre. Be quick!'

Outside, the iron gate creaked open, followed by the noise of soldiers breaking in, some rushing upstairs, some searching the courtyard. 'Where does that gate lead to?' I heard the familiar voice of von den Velde.

'The cloistered garden. Only the nuns are allowed...'

'Open it!'

'Never!'

'Breche das Tor! Mach schnell!'

Paolo's strong hands pushed me down hard into the tunnel. 'Here, Padre, the envelope!' I heard the gun shots aimed at the lock. Before I was able to utter a word of protest, the wooden plank was slid over me, heaps of earth fell on it, and then the heavy stones were pushed into place. As I moved forward in complete darkness, I heard hurried footsteps in the garden and the clicking of gun bolts.

After a while all sounds faded behind me. I had to stoop or crouch down, groping with my hands to find my way. Occasionally, I could hear panting or would bump into someone. Finally I discerned the outline of a man's bowed back and a small sliver of light ahead told me I was nearing the end of the passage. A moment later I crawled out in a barren, wintry field, where part of my Jewish flock awaited me in the huge shadows of the ancient, gnarled olive trees.

I turned my head. In the pale moonlight I could see silhouettes of many men already climbing the steep ground, disappearing among the rocks and undergrowth, making for the forest of Monte Subasio as we had planned. Those who remained were the elderly who were unable to climb, and they waited for me to take them to San Damiano. I knew that at this very moment other groups of Jews who had left their monasteries at the sound of the warning bells were making for the same destination, where they hoped the twenty guerillas could offer them some protection and where they might hide in the almost impenetrable forest or find refuge with peasants.

'Come, my children,' I said to men twice my age.

And I began to lead my group down to San Damiano, so that they could join the other Jews hiding there in monks' habits.

The next day I learned from Franca what had happened at San Quirico after we left. The German soldiers rushed past Franca and Paolo into the outhouse, while von den Velde, flicking his baton, approached the couple. 'Are you a nun?' he asked the girl, mockingly. He glanced at Gay, motioned to one of his men to guard him, then entered the outhouse. His eyes passed over the rows of stripped beds and then Franca saw him move further into the room. She followed. The Captain approached a bed in the corner, where somehow a small caseless pillow had been forgotten. He touched it. 'Warm,' he said, then he turned to her. 'Who slept here?'

She rushed to him. 'Captain, please,' she whispered. 'It's me—and him. Don't tell the nuns, they would be furious.'

Captain von den Velde's face broke into a smile. 'I see.' He passed through the next room and found the door to the convent building closed. He returned to Franca. 'And how did you get in?'

'Over the wall. We're both staying at the guest-house.'

The Captain went back to the garden. 'Your papers,' he said to Gay. Paolo dug out the envelope from inside his shirt and handed it over. 'Bring him in,' the SS officer ordered and then went out and up the staircase. A soldier followed, his gun aimed at Paolo Gay as he walked upstairs to the hall of the guest-house. Franca followed. 'The guest book,' von den Velde said to Suora Beata who was behind the reception desk. Meanwhile some Nazi soldiers and the OVRA men were pushing people out of the rooms and lining them up in the hall. There were a few men and women, some elderly, and children in their night-shirts or pyjamas. It was at this very moment that Mother Giuseppina charged in out of the parlour, followed by Suora Amata who had run to fetch her from the cloister. 'How dare you?' she began. 'This is a convent. We're daughters of God...'

'Halt's Maul!' the Captain said, and his men laughed. 'What are you keeping those beds in there for?' He motioned in the direction of the outhouse.

'For our guests,' Suora Amata said quickly, to take upon herself the burden of lying. 'In case we have an influx of guests. But, unfortunately,' she signed, 'we don't. We depend on the guest-house for our income, you know.'

Mother Giuseppina, who ignored the German's rudeness, approached the Captain. 'This is a cloister. A secluded cloister!'

'This is a haven for anti-Fascists,' von den Velde replied in Italian, hitting his baton on the reception desk.

'Will you leave, please, at once! Or I'll call the Bishop!'

'Call the Pope if you like,' the SS officer said, then sharply pulled the big key hanging from the Mother Abbess's belt. It broke off. The Mother Abbess gasped in horror. Von den Velde handed the key to an SS man. 'Check all the cells of the cloister!' Then, as a few of his soldiers rushed out of the room, he calmly started to read the register. The people in the hall, scared out of their wits, replied as their names were called out. The Captain closed the book. 'You don't have either a Paolo Macri, nor Antonio Podda, nor...'

'Yes, we do,' Suora Amata said firmly. Her hands trembling, she picked up the book, opened it, her eyes scanning the pages. 'Oh, it must have been an oversight... They were staying here and they didn't return tonight.'

'They are in Perugia prison, awaiting execution.'

'What for? What have they done?' It was Franca who screamed.

'On the night of 22 February a Fascist priest was shot in Foligno. By a Slav. Was Paolo Macri here on the night of 22 February?'

'Of course. We played checkers together that evening. What else can one do during curfew?'

Von den Velde looked at her with the glint of a smile, and Franca blushed. The officer's eyes glided over to Paolo Gay and the sight of the tall, blond man, made him finally open the envelope. He looked over the identity card, the army draft release, the ration book, then he picked up the register. 'You are not registered here either,' he said.

An OVRA man came to the captain, pushed his sun-glasses onto his forehead and glanced at the documents. 'Good God!' he said. 'We have been looking for this man for months. This is Colonel Gay, ex-member of the Italian Army's General Staff—a deserter and a traitor!'

Paolo's face grew instantly ashen. 'What do you mean? I am not.'

'Of course,' von den Velde said, 'that's what your papers say.' He handed the ID card to Gay. 'Right?'

'Dio!' Paolo whispered. 'Dio mio!' He dug his fingers into his eyes in a gesture of utter despair. In the rush to let everyone escape and to cover the exit, he had given me the wrong envelope—the one containing the forged papers, and had now handed to the German his real ones.

At this very moment the soldiers came back from searching the cloister. Their leader shook his head. Hauptsturmführer von den Velde whipped his Lüger out of its leather holster and pointed the gun at Gay.

'Take him to Bastia,' he said. 'I'll deliver him personally to Perugia in the morning.'

Together with Fra Euralio I led my group through our vineyards into the caves of the hill of San Feliciano. It was safer for them to spend the rest of the night in hiding. Tomorrow we would dress them in habits and begin to teach them how to behave and pray as monks, as we had taught so many others.

As we were returning, we saw a gaunt, stooped man working his way across the flagged road towards our monastery. I recognised Professor Fano. He came over to us and for a moment just looked at me, speechless, trying to catch his breath. Then he said, 'They came to St Colette—the Nazis and the OVRA; they broke into the cloister. We managed to get out in time. The others have fled into the mountains, but I had no strength left and so I came here.'

'Father Euralio will guide you to a safe place, Maestro,' I said. 'Until the morning, until the danger has passed.'

The two men started, but after a few steps the grey-haired old man turned. 'All my life I've felt Italian, as my ancestors did for centuries.' Sadly, he shook his head. 'No longer, no longer...'

A moment later I saw him and Fra Euralio disappear into the darkness.

With a heavy heart I flung myself on to a bench in the courtyard, oblivious of the cold wind blowing in from the mountains. There, a score of men, women and children were braving that wind, braving the winter, carrying their meagre belongings up towards the area of the Hermitage and the Abbey of San Benedetto, no longer people, but hunted animals looking for an escape. In one single night our entire work had been shattered and all the monasteries emptied of refugees, except for those disguised as monks. Until now, with the end of the war almost in sight, we had managed to provide a safe haven for these Jews. Perhaps today, perhaps tomorrow, von den Velde and his henchmen would go up to Mount Subasio, penetrate the forest and pluck down, one by one, all those who had managed to stay alive until now.

Desperately, I rushed into the church and knelt before the altar crucifix. 'Oh, God!' I cried. 'Where are You when Your chosen people, when we, Your sons and daughters, who have served You faithfully all our lives, are begging for Your help? Where are You in our desperate hour of need?' Then with a sudden wave of remorse I prostrated my face and body on the cold floor. 'Oh, God, merciful God, forgive me for questioning You!' For a while I said no more, but my head was bursting. We peasants are more down to earth than anyone and I, Salvatore Rufino Niccacci, a peasant turned priest, have the right to ask. We Christians have the Cross. The Nazis came and turned that Cross into a swastika. Why did You let them profane You? And what about Your deputy on earth? Why does he keep silent? Our Pope's condemnation of the Nazis would perhaps make every third one of the German soldiers stop killing, at least stop killing the innocent. Isn't his role as the spiritual leader of the Church more important than his role of politician or head of state? What comfort he could give to all those now hiding in the mountains and caves if he would only stand up for them openly and thus strengthen their will to live, hide, and survive. Has he done enough by quietly letting his subordinates help those that are being persecuted? Couldn't he have done more? And shouldn't You, Almighty, in this greatest hour of our need, have given us a leader who would have stood up to the devil who twisted Your Cross?

I raised myself to my knees and folded my hands in prayer. 'God, merciful God, forgive us our trespasses as we forgive Yours.' Then I beat my chest with my fist. 'Mea culpa, mea maxima culpa,' I said and I might have gone on and on raving like this if the noise of shuffling feet had not reached me.

I looked out and saw in the first bluish light of dawn the monks walking towards the church. It was too early for lauds and when the men entered I recognised our Jewish refugees and realised that though they usually followed our lauds with their morning minyan they had this time come earlier, to pray for their God's protection in their hour of peril.

At the first sound of Hebrew I got up, to move tactfully away, when I suddenly heard a car and saw the military Volkswagen racing towards the church. I recognised von den Velde at the wheel, and next to him—Colonel Müller. The moment the car came to a stop, three SS men, with guns in their hands, jumped out and ran towards us. My heart skipped a beat and my stomach turned cold. All the Jews froze in their places; it was impossible to escape now. But, as always in a crisis, I quickly recovered, started the mass, and heard the men behind me immediately switching to Latin and lustily repeating Kyrie eleison, Christe eleison, Kyrie eleison.

The soldiers halted right outside the entry to the church, uneasily glancing back at their officers. I continued the mass and my congregation echoed my prayers with their responses.

'Sorry to interrupt your service, Padre,' I heard von den Velde's voice from the door. He held his baton under his arm. 'I want my men to search the monastery. It will only take a minute.' And, without waiting for my approval, he signalled to his three armed men and they rushed into the inner quarters of the cloister.

I walked straight down the aisle, to face the SS chief. 'I don't understand,' I said. 'What's the reason for this search?' I looked at Colonel Müller, accustomed to his support. But his face was immobile, with no trace of its usual friendliness. 'Your nuns', he said frostily, 'gave refuge to our enemies. And the four men you tried to intercede for yesterday are anti-German partisans.'

'I'm sure they are not, Colonel.' My voice rose in indignation. 'The Lord Bishop has asked Fortini to defend them. It will all be cleared up at the trial.'

'*If* there is a trial,' von den Velde said with a smile. Then he walked into the cloister to supervise the search.

'I don't understand, Colonel,' I said. 'How could you, a Catholic, let them violate our cloister?'

He grimaced. 'This was Hauptsturmführer von den Velde's order, not mine.'

'But you're his superior, you could oppose it. He's only a captain.'

'Yes, but a captain of the SS.' Then, almost with a sadness, he added, 'I trusted you, Padre. Completely. You have abused my trust.' And before I could say anything more, he walked away to meet von den Velde and his soldiers coming out of the cloister. 'Gar nichts,' the SS chief said. 'Alles ist in Ordnung.'

He saluted and so did the Colonel. Within a minute they were in their car and gone, without so much as a word of apology.

I smiled for the first time since yesterday afternoon, and all the men in the church breathed sighs of relief. Then, when I walked back to the altar crucifix, with a heavy burden of guilt and the tremendous need to apologise to my Saviour, I heard the people behind me resume their morning service. 'Heavenly Master,' they were praying in unison, swaying piously, and just as they knew the meaning of Christian prayers, I by now knew what they were saying. 'At the dawn of a new day hear our voice. Thou art the source of our strength.'

I could do no less than they. From the cloister came my Christian brothers, walking in pairs to their lauds. I approached the altar. 'In the hour of my trouble', I said, 'I sought the Lord. My hand was stretched out in the night.' And then I added on my own, 'And He responded. He responded!'

XV

High up in the dense oak forest of Monte Subasio, St Francis and his companions had found caves where they lived like hermits and spent their days in penitence and contemplation, regaining their strength. Now our refugees were hiding there. I and several of my brothers reached the place at 4 p.m., after an hour's strenuous climb. Occasionally from behind a holm-oak we heard a word of greeting from an armed partisan, a number of whom were now guarding the approaches to the Hermitage Convent, where we had arranged to meet representatives of the refugee families. As soon as we entered the courtyard, they came out of their hiding-place to meet us, anxious to get news of what had happened in the night and what they were to do next.

Fortini had told the Bishop that none of the men in Perugia had been executed. Rocchi and von den Velde had brought in Paolo Gay, and the five were now in separate cells, being interrogated continuously. We had no idea whether they were being tortured or if any of them had broken down. We were told, though, that the Gestapo and the OVRA had hoped to extract from them details of where the others were hiding. And of course, since those arrested, except for young Fano, were all members of our San Quirico headquarters, they knew those details.

A young seminarist who had come with me handed me a list. It contained the names of peasants living in remote places in the surrounding countryside and also a number of names of inhabitants of Assisi willing to accept more Catholic refugees. Those who did not look Jewish were directed to the town; those who did, into the mountains. All day long, the monks and priests of Assisi tried to find homes for them, and still we didn't have enough room for everybody. Return to the convents was out of the question. They were now the most suspect of all hiding-places. But I was ready to accept a few more, men of course, and the Bishop himself volunteered to take in at least thirty people, men, women and children, to be hidden not only in his legnaia but also in the numerous Roman ruins in the Palace grounds. In case of alarm, the refugees at the Bishop's Palace and mine would have plenty of time to escape to the near-by fields and hide in caves.

As soon as I had read out the name of a family, one of my brothers was designated to accompany the head of that family to collect and guide them to their new accommodation. Finally, only four of the refugees remained: Nino Maionica, the two Americans and Albert Finzi. The Americans stopped me before I was ready to tell them where they were going. Frank raised his hand. 'Father,' he announced in English and Nino translated, 'Danny and I are both joining the partisans. They are leaderless now; we shall offer them our military expertise.'

'All right,' I said, 'if that's what you wish to do.'

'Yes,' Frank answered in his strange Texas drawl. 'That's what we wish to do.'

And as soon as Nino completed the translation, he himself added, 'And that's what I wish to do, too. As soon as I've seen to it that all the Maionicas are safe.'

'Good. Signor Finzi, we have a place for you in the grounds of the Bishop's Palace.'

'I'm afraid it won't do,' he said. He was a gaunt, erect man with blue eyes. 'You see, my wife is expecting a baby any day now. We can't get her to a hospital, nor can she have the baby at the Bishop's Palace, can she?'

I had forgotten. I had seen his attractive, raven-haired wife, Marie, at St Colette, growing bigger by the day. She was a daughter of the former Burgomaster of Antwerp, he was of Slav origin, and they had a two-year old daughter, Brigitte.

The sun was sinking behind the mountain now. Everybody else had left. Through the steep paths of the forest my brothers were now guiding the Jews to their new hiding-places. I could do no less. In addition, I knew what Albert Finzi did not know. The OVRA men were looking for him. Somehow they had learned his name and they must have mistaken it for another Finzi, a descendant of an Italian patriot and supporter of Garibaldi, who had spent a few days in Assisi and left after receiving his papers. Forged documents with the Italian name Figuccia could not fool the OVRA if they ever caught this man with his heavy foreign accent.

'Where are your wife and child?' I asked.

'Not far away. Half a kilometre from here.'

'Padre,' I said to one of the monks of the Hermitage, 'do you have a horse and cart?'

The bearded man looked at me bewildered. 'Yes,' he said. 'What for?'

'I shall return it tomorrow. Have the horse harnessed.'

It was now Finzi's turn to look perplexed. 'Where are we going?' he asked.

'To Deruta,' I said. 'To my home. My brother's home and mine.'

I shall never forget that night. From a well hidden cave we picked up Marie and little Brigitte. Darkness enveloped us as I drove down the mountain. Below, I could see the sharp outlines of the Basilicas of Santa Maria degli Angeli and St Francis, and the Great and Small Forts rising majestically into the sombre sky. When we reached the foot of Monte Subasio, I turned the cart on to the narrow paths which crossed the fields, away from the villages and German patrols. Marie held her little girl asleep in her arms, her head resting against her husband's shoulder, the three of them shivering under one blanket. After a while the man and the woman lapsed into an upright, restless doze, exhausted after the previous night's escape and hiding in the cold cave. Only the horse and I were awake, under the wintry sky lit only by the pale moonlight, as we rode on our three-hour trek to the house of my childhood, where another child was shortly to be born.

The interrogations at Perugia lasted for three days and three nights. At one point Giorgio, so sure of himself when free, but terrified of being tortured in jail, tried to throw himself from the third floor down the staircase but Bruno Fano grabbed him by the arms. On 29 February 1944—this was a leap year—the last of the interrogations was completed. Criminal action was recommended against Gay for high treason, against Podda for avoiding the army call-up, and against Kropf, Jozsa and Fano for acquiring false documents. The charge against Pali of taking part in the assassination of the Foligno priest was dismissed; the charge that the others were active partisans was dropped. Not for a single moment did either Rocchi or von den Velde suspect that they had three Jews in their custody.

The men were transferred to a jail, which had once been a women's prison. White-clad nuns still served the prisoners their food and gave them religious solace. Their ordeal was not over. They were thrown each into a different cell. Each cell was small, with some twenty-five people crammed into it—deserters, criminals, political prisoners—so that there was no room to lie down; the one meal of the day consisted of gruel, bread and barley coffee. Prisoners were called at random and their interrogations continued. And every day at 5 a.m. there was a rap at the door; a burly Gestapo sergeant with two Italian guards would enter and pick one or two men from each cell, to be shot, without trial, as a warning to the others, to make them try to save their lives by divulging any information they had about the enemies of the Third Reich and the Republic of Salo. Physical torture was not necessary; waiting fearfully for 5 a.m. every day and the sergeant's slow scrutiny of the men lined up in front of him was enough. Rocchi and van den Velde were patient.

About two weeks later I plucked up courage to call on Colonel Müller. I had to do something to help our men.

It was a pleasant, warm day, with the promise of spring in the air, when I entered the Hotel Subasio. But I did not go directly to his office because the memory of our last encounter at San Damiano was still too vivid. I asked Andrea Rossi at the reception desk to announce me over the phone. He picked up the receiver. I watched him as he gave my name, then waited for a reply; his face registered the change in the German officer's attitude towards me. 'The Colonel', he said after putting the phone down, 'is very sorry, but he is extremely busy.'

'Oh, well, it can happen,' I managed to say, and waved cheerfully and left. This is it, I thought to myself as I walked back home, my head bowed dejectedly. We were no longer under the protection of Colonel Müller, only under the protection of the Wehrmacht. On the Via San Francesco, right on the walls of the house where Don Brunacci lived, I saw a new poster, stating that the reward for denouncing a Jew or an anti-Fascist had been raised from a thousand to five thousand lire. A company of Blackshirts, waving black flags and singing 'Giovinezza', marched past. For the first time in Assisi I became afraid when a car suddenly stopped behind me, at the thought of a stranger coming up to tap me on the shoulder. But when I reached the Piazza del Comune and saw people sitting peacefully in the open-air cafés and heard the turtle-doves cooing from the roof of the Palace of the Captain of the People, I decided to stop at the Minerva for a glass of wine, hoping it would cheer me up.

When I had downed my second glass, I saw Cardelli swaggering from his home across the piazza towards the café. He spotted me and waved. I returned a lame salute. He quickened his pace and sat down at my table.

'I just heard on my radio', he whispered, 'that the Russians have crossed the Bug river into Poland. The Allied invasion of Europe cannot be far off now.'

Just as he called for his wine, little Brizi in his black borsalino emerged from the Corso Mazzini. His face, too, was all smiles. He reached our table and pulled out a chair to join us. 'The Germans came to my store,' he said. 'Two armed Gestapo men. They went straight into the printing shop and searched for discarded type and rubber seals.' When the waiter appeared, Luigi raised his fingers. 'A whole carafe! On me!' he ordered, in an unusual gesture of generosity. He turned back to us. 'Well, they found nothing incriminating.'

Since the razzia of 26 February, Brizi & Brizi were no longer printing false documents. Cardinal della Costa and the relay stations between Florence and Assisi were no longer sending us Jews. Assisi had become as dangerous a place to be in as any other town.

The wine was put on our table and three glasses filled. 'And you know something?' Luigi chuckled, lifting his glass. 'When the Gestapo were leaving, my Trento called them back. "How about a majolica relief of St Francis? Or some postcards for your family?" he asked, innocently. The Germans, guilt-stricken about the unwarranted raid, bought two postcards.' Luigi burst out laughing. 'Views of San Damiano and San Quirico!' We joined him in his laughter. 'The one good thing, Padre Rufino,' he added, 'is that I can now finally catch up on my sleep. Not a single Jewish refugee has come to our area in weeks.'

Luigi Brizi was wrong. The very same afternoon I was called to the phone. It was urgent, I was told. I walked nervously out of my cell. We had avoided communicating by phone—all telephones were being monitored by the OVRA. I picked up the receiver. Enrico, my brother, was at the other end of the line, calling from a Deruta public phone booth. 'It's a boy!' he shouted.

'What?' I asked, bewildered.

'A boy. Signora Finzi gave birth to a boy last night. Tonight we celebrate. Come over. We're preparing a feast. And they've decided to call the boy Enrico, after me.'

'Give them my very best wishes. I'll be there, and I'll walk if I have to!' And, later that day, I did indeed walk for two hours, to welcome a new Jewish arrival to the Assisi area.

It was wonderful to be back home, with my family, to hear again the soft rush of our stream, the creak of the watermill, the happy babble of children and the pleasant crackle of firewood from the kitchen stove. My sister-in-law Maria was not only a good midwife—she had delivered the baby some twelve hours earlier—she was also a good cook. So, after seeing the baby and kissing the beaming mother on her head, I was ushered to a long table in the dining-room, covered with home-spun white linen tablecloth and set with the Deruta ceramic plates that my village had been producing for the past six centuries. My eldest brother Luigi was holding a huge carafe of wine, filling the glasses, full for the men, a finger-breadth for the children. The moment he saw Albert Finzi, he guided him, paying no heed to the man's protests, to his own honoured place at the head of the table.

As soon as the adults had sat down and the children, including little Brigitte, had been made comfortable, Luigi's wife brought in a tureen of steaming pea soup. With gusto we dipped our home-made bread in it, and, when we'd finished, in came the *pièce de résistance*—pollo del faraone, two roast birds that Maria carried proudly to the table on a silver platter. They had been shot only a few hours earlier for the occasion by her husband, who had risked someone hearing the shots. The use of hunting guns was strictly forbidden, but this is where we always got our meat—from the air. Attracted by the grain and water, the wild faraoni flew often over our land. My sister-in-law busied herself with serving us. We ate and drank and laughed as people do on birthdays in peacetime. It was only a pity that the real heroine of the event had to stay in bed and could not be with us, but she got a good trayful, and we drank to her health and the baby's health as many times as to that of Albert. Then, eager to contribute something, I passed my cigarettes around, and we all smoked with our barley coffee, as Maria finally sat down and had her own meal.

Suddenly we heard a car. The laughter ceased immediately, glasses and cigarettes froze in our hands. Enrico got up and walked to the door. 'The OVRA!' he whispered into the room.

I looked at Luigi. 'Don't worry,' he said, 'the gun is well hidden in the mill.'

A moment later, with a clipped 'Buona sera', two men in sun-glasses entered. Their jackets were open and we could see revolvers stuck in leather holsters. 'Which of you is Alberto Finzi?' a sleek man with a thin moustache asked. He barely glanced at the table. The blood drained from the face of our guest of honour. He put his glass down and heavily rose from his chair. 'I am.'

'Please come with us.'

'Where to?' Finzi muttered.

'To the Questura. In Perugia.'

'What for?' I interceded.

'Interrogation.'

I moved towards the man. 'You can't do that. His wife has just had a baby. This very morning. You can see. Come along, I'll show you.'

'Congratulations,' the man said tartly. 'Sorry, Padre, we have our orders.' He put his hand on his revolver.

We watched helplessly as Albert went into his room to bid his wife and child goodbye. We heard a sudden sob and at the sound of her mother's cry little Brigitte started too and ran to her. I wanted to scream, threaten the men with God's punishment, but my better judgement told me to keep my mouth shut. After a while Albert returned with a small bundle—underwear, socks, a shirt. But he tried to keep composed and dignified; only his eyes betrayed his feelings. He shook our hands. 'Take care of my wife and children,' he said. Brigitte ran back into the room, throwing her arms around her father's neck as if trying to hold him back. He kissed her and managed a few reassuring words. 'I am ready,' he said to the OVRA men.

'Tomorrow, Albert, I shall ask the Lord Bishop to intervene,' I said, trying in turn to reassure him. 'I'm sure he will succeed.' I was only too aware of the hollow sound of my voice.

The three men left. We heard the car depart. My family looked at me searchingly. I, as a man of the cloth, was supposed to know how to console people. I took Brigitte by the hand and brought her to her mother. But I remained silent, unable to offer any false promises. With a heavy heart I looked at the grief-stricken woman, her frightened little girl, and her new-born baby peacefully sleeping in a cradle. Only two weeks earlier, I thought, I had driven them to what I had hoped to be the safest of all places. Perhaps no longer was there such a place. The Gestapo and the OVRA had now taken six of our men. I wondered who would be next.

I found out much sooner than I expected. When at about midnight I emerged from the grove of olive trees and stepped on to the gravel road leading to San Damiano, I saw the familiar Volkswagen waiting in front of the monastery gate, less than fifty metres away. Instinctively I stepped back, but it was too late. Von den Velde, standing beside his car, had noticed me. 'Good evening, Padre,' he said in a loud, mocking tone. I walked slowly towards him. At the wheel sat an SS man. 'I see you believe that the curfew does not apply to you.'

'I was called to christen a baby in my home town, Deruta.'

'Pity you didn't tell me. I would gladly have provided you with transport, the way Colonel Müller did.' He opened the car door and waved his baton invitingly. 'Please.' My stomach turned cold. I saw von den Velde's face breaking into a self-satisfied smile. 'We're going to Bastia,' he announced. 'A little ride and a chat should do us both good.'

Sorrowfully, I glanced at my monastery, knowing that none of my brothers, my Christian and Jewish brothers, was asleep. I wondered whether I would ever see them, whether I would ever see San Damiano again.

XVI

Hauptsturmführer Ernst von den Velde settled himself in an armchair, under the portrait of his Führer and a Swastika flag. He pointed to a chair. I sat down and nervously pulled out my packet of cigarettes. No word had been exchanged between us on the way to Bastia. 'Here, Padre,' the Captain said, opening a silver box. 'They're better. German.' He flicked on his golden lighter and lit my cigarette, then his own.

The room was in a former military barracks, plaster chipping from its whitewashed walls. On the desk I noticed a photograph of a woman and a boy with remarkably similar features, and an equestrian statue with a plaque reading 'Baron Ernst von den Velde. First prize. Baden-Baden, 1939.' So he was a family man and an aristocrat, two things I had not known about him. The Captain caught my look, inhaled deeply, then said amiably, 'I am really a cavalryman, but they don't have much use for horses in this war, I am afraid, so here I am trying to serve my country in another capacity.' He straightened the pile of papers on his desk and opened the top folder. I sensed that, after the pleasant introductory talk, the interrogation was about to begin. I shifted in my chair, but then, helpfully, the words of the Bishop echoed through my head, reminding me of his trust that I would not lose my head when questioned by the Gestapo.

'I want to reassure you, Padre,' von den Velde said, leaning forward and crossing his palms in mocking imitation of my habitual gesture, 'that I am not a less considerate man than Colonel Müller. Only, perhaps, less gullible. You see, I am not a Catholic. So now let's get down to business, shall we?' He looked at his papers and his voice acquired the professional, cold tone of an interrogator. 'You brought a man called Alberto Figuccia to your home in Deruta?'

'Correct.'

'He was interrogated tonight. We suspected that he was in fact Finzi, a Jew and an active anti-Fascist. We now know that he speaks with a foreign accent, and is not the man we were looking for. But neither is he Italian. Obviously he has forged papers.'

'As far as I know, Captain,' I interrupted, 'he is a Belgian citizen, a war refugee.'

'Figucia is an Italian name.'

I put my hands on the desk. 'And are Skorzeny, Wishnevski, Novak, German names?' I retorted. 'Their ancestors were Slav and Figuccia's ancestors may have been Italian for all I know.'

The Captain lined up the row of razor-sharpened pencils in front of him. 'Colonel Gay,' he said. 'A former member of the General Staff of the Italian Army. And Lieutenant Podda, an Air Force officer. One a traitor, the other a deserter. Do you know them?'

I threw my hands up in a gesture of extreme shock. 'What? I had no idea that they were officers. Of course I know them; they stayed at the San Quirico guest-house.'

'How do you know that, Padre? They were not listed in the register. Do you visit San Quirico often?'

'Of course I do. I take care of the spiritual needs of the refugees from the south, and I also happen to be father confessor to some of the nuns.'

Von den Velde tightened his lips. 'We're going to execute them, you know?'

'You should,' I said indignantly. 'Traitors should be executed.'

For a moment he looked studiously at me through his narrowed eyes. 'Now—another name. Paolo Jozsa, a Slav who was also living at the guest-house. Also not registered. Since you knew everyone there, you must have known him too.'

'I didn't say I knew everyone there. I am Father Superior of San Damiano, not Mother Superior of San Quirico.'

The Captain cracked an artificial smile. 'Very funny! Now—perhaps you knew the man under the name of Paolo Macri?'

'This sounds more familiar. But I... No, I'm not sure I met him personally.'

From his folder von den Velde picked up a copy of the record of the interrogation of Pali and put it in front of me. He rubbed his little moustache, watching me attentively as I read that the accused, Paolo Macri, had admitted that this was not his true name and that he had acquired his documents from one Petar

Marinovich on an Assisi street for the sum of 3,000 lire. He did it because in the war he had lost his own papers. I shrugged. 'I have never met anyone called Marinovich, nor do I believe that I ever met—what was his name again?'

'It's written further down the document. Paolo Jozsa.'

'You said he is a Slav? Perhaps he belongs to the Eastern Orthodox Church?' I volunteered. 'In that case he would have had no reason to seek my spiritual help.'

The German officer fixed me with his eyes, but I did not blink. Then he picked up another paper for me to look at. It said there that when the individual in possession of an identity card bearing the name of Giorgio Cianura was about to sign the transcript of his interrogation, he started with writing 'Kro', then blotted it with ink before writing his full name. 'Do you know what his real name was', von den Velde's voice rang with mockery, 'before *he* acquired new documents from Petar Marinovich or anyone else on an Assisi street?' The Captain quickly tried to remove the paper from my hand, perhaps too quickly, so I had time to notice that Giorgio had explained that this was his nickname.

I let go of the document. 'I met the man,' I said. 'If I recall, he is from Brindisi or a little town near-by.'

'Francavilla Fontana,' von den Velde said helpfully, reading from the interrogation.

'I believe he told me he used to call himself "Kro" as a child and the nickname just stuck.'

Von den Velde, irritated, got up from behind his desk and walked to the window. Through it I could see a helmeted and armed sentry pacing back and forth. 'You are a clever man, Padre,' the Captain said; 'perhaps too clever for a peasant from Deruta.' When he turned I noticed for the first time a nervous twitch in the corner of his mouth.

'I'm only trying to be of some assistance to you,' I said, my confidence boosted further.

The Captain returned to his desk and picked up the next document. 'This is the transcript of the interrogation of Lieutenant Antonio Podda,' he said. His finger pointed to a line that said that among Podda's papers had been found the scribbled name of 'one Padre Rufino Miccacci and the telephone number of San Damiano'. 'Could you tell me how this name came into his possession, unless you were to serve as some contact with the enemy or the partisans?'

'I have no idea,' I said. 'I also have some names and phone numbers.' I pulled out my wallet, dug out a slip of paper and handed it over to him. It read, 'Colonel Müller. Telephone 210.'

In a fury Captain von den Velde grabbed his baton and hit his desk. 'Are you trying to make a fool out of me?' he said. 'I'm not Colonel Müller, you know! All right!' Abruptly, he sat down. 'Let's stop playing games. How many refugees are there in Assisi?'

'I don't know. You probably know better.'

'You know,' he said. 'Two thousand. And how many of these are anti-Fascists? And how many Jews? And how many have forged papers?' I remained silent, just shaking my head, as if dumbfounded by his insinuations. He now jumped up again from his seat, and sat on the desk. 'You think, Padre, that you can hide behind that habit of yours? We know all about your movements—we have our informers in town and they are generously rewarded for each useful piece of information. You think we don't know that many of the so-called refugees staying at various convent guest-houses vanished just before we got to them? Which means, of course, that you have your informers, too. Well, Padre, let's see which of us has the better ones, eh?' He clenched his fist and then grabbed me by my shoulder and shook me hard. 'I'm going to smash you and your underground in no time, you'll see! And I won't rest until I do!'

I have never seen a man change so suddenly. His face went red, sweat appeared on his forehead, his mouth twitched. 'The Catholic clergy is our enemy,' he said. 'We have shot three thousand priests in Europe so far. Do you think we will hesitate a moment before putting one more in front of the firing squad?'

He went to the door and yelled, 'Get him out of here and into solitary. No food, no water! And let him rot there!' He shouted his order in Italian and then I saw an OVRA man with a holstered pistol enter. Apparently a few of them were attached to the Gestapo. 'Come!' said the man, pointing the way in front of him. I got up, hearing behind me 'Zum Teufel!' and the sharp, angry snapping of von den Velde's baton against his desk.

I was used to sleeping in a small cell on an iron bed and a coarse mattress, but not under a glaring bulb. Nor was my cell at San Damiano locked from the outside. I sat down and looked around; there was nothing else in the room except a tin bucket in the corner into which the prisoner could relieve himself. A barred window faced the walled courtyard and behind it a soldier, rifle slung, appeared and disappeared every minute. I lay down, put my arm under my head and tried to examine my situation.

The Captain had plenty of suspicions, but apparently no hard evidence. The men in Perugia had stood up well to their ordeal. He could easily have shot any one of us; it was a Nazi war with Nazi rules and they often executed people without any proof of guilt. It was not my confession that von den Velde was after; he wanted the exposure of our entire underground, so that as many people as possible could be rounded up and shot. He wanted another trophy for his record, the triumph of a captain over his gullible superior, perhaps an advancement, a medal or maybe even an appreciation from Reichsführer SS Himmler himself.

I looked at my watch. It was two o'clock. I needed all the strength, not only spiritual but also physical, that I could get. I closed my eyes, but still felt the light blazing through my eyelids. I turned away from it to the wall and with the discipline I had learned as a monk forced myself to fall asleep.

I was awakened by noise from the courtyard—soldiers were running, I heard an officer's call to attention, the checking of rifle magazines, more sounds of hurrying feet and then the Italian names of prisoners being called out by the Germans. I got up and went to the window. It was still dark, but a truck was roaring in through an open gate and coming to a stop. Then I saw four men and two women, their hands raised, being forced by armed guards into the truck. As soon as they had clambered aboard, the soldiers followed them and an OVRA man took his place next to the driver. The vehicle turned around, its headlights blinding me momentarily, and as it drove towards the gate a woman's shrill voice pierced the night: 'I haven't done anything! I am not guilty!' The soldiers shut the gate, the sound of the motor slowly faded and then there was silence.

I lay back on the bed, wide awake, haunted by what I had heard. A fly kept buzzing around the naked bulb. Outside my window, the sentry was pacing back and forth with maddening regularity. I waited anxiously for the dawn, hoping that soon my brothers at San Damiano would alert the Bishop, and that the Bishop would alert Cardinal della Costa. Then my hopes faded, for I realised that even the Pope himself was powerless before a captain of the SS.

The morning brought again the noise of the vehicles and soldiers arriving and departing and the distant tolling of church bells for the lauds. I knocked at the door. There was no answer. I started banging on it. Finally, I heard the key turn, the door creaked open and the face of a German guard appeared. 'I want a crucifix in my room,' I said. The soldier looked at me, not understanding a word, then snapped 'Kein Essen!' and shut the door in my face. I wasn't longing for food—the sumptuous meal of last night would last me for quite a while—but I wanted to take part in lauds. I pulled out the chain hanging round my neck, cradled the cross in my palm, then knelt down by the bed and buried my head in my hands.

When I had finished praying, I took a walk in my cell, at first calm and refreshed by my prayers, but then the five steps to the window and five back to the wall became more and more brisk and irritated. After an hour of aimless pacing, I lay down again, then got up again and went once more to the window, peering out at the now empty courtyard, its tall walls and a sliver of sky above them. Then, to pass the time, I counted—twenty-five from the time the senty disappeared from my view until he reappeared. I never saw the man's face because he always passed very close to my window. I never knew if that face changed, though once at midday it must have, because my count went up to seventy before the soldier reappeared. The bells rang for the nones prayers and I could clearly distinguish the chimes of the Basilica of Santa Maria degli Angeli. After fifteen years I knew them all by heart. Once more

I knelt and prayed and then pulled out my breviary and read.

With the prayers coming to their inevitable end, with the fly still stubbornly buzzing in the room, I discovered that I had begun waiting, hoping for a knock at the door and a call for my next interrogation, anything to relieve the nerve-shattering monotony. But the door never opened, not even in the afternoon when I begun to get hungry and thirsty, after my last two cigarettes had been smoked, nor during the short nap which I hoped would somehow shorten what had been the longest day of my life. Then suddenly, when I had started to walk the room again, it dawned on me that von den Velde would really stick to his word. I would rot in this cell until I agreed to tell all. Outside, the sentry kept pacing the ground; inside my cell, I paced the floor with a more and more stubborn resolve to keep step with him.

Relief came when the bells began to ring. I looked through my window. Above the courtyard wall I saw a streak of sky turning into the brilliant red of departing day. But this time, perhaps because I was standing at the window, or perhaps because I was straining my ears, the bells seemed to come from many directions and in my mind I could see Umbrian peasants and townsfolk filling the churches, the men well dressed, the women with lace-covered heads, holding their children by the hand, the choirboys in white, helping in the ceremony. I could smell the incense and see the red-cassocked priest blessing the people with the sign of the cross, and could hear his prayers and his congregation's responses. There I was, vicariously participating in another canonical hour of the day, in solitary confinement, between the only two homes I had ever known, bearing my cross, on my own road to Calvary.

Night passed into day and day into night, with the light blinding me, with only the grey or black of the window and the toll of the bells telling me what time it was. No one ever entered the room, either to bring me food or drink, or even to empty the toilet bucket. I fell into a sort of numbed stupor, relieved only by prayers and lapses into childhood memories. Each night prisoners were collected and driven off, presumably to a place of execution. I would sit up in bed in a panic to listen to the calling of the names, and only after the truck had departed would I lie down again and sink back into a restless sleep.

Sometimes in the day I would shake off my apathy, make for the door and bang my fist against it, pleading, screaming for a drink. After a while the guard would show his face and ask 'Hauptsturmführer, sprechen?' And when I said no, no, all I wanted was a glass of water, he would shut the door again.

On the third night, when I was once more awakened by an engine roaring, a uniformed figure appeared at my window, and bent down so that I could see his face. 'Rufino Salvatore Niccacci!' I heard. A cold shiver ran down my spine as I listened to the key being turned in my door. 'Raus!' The rifle butt pushed me forward to where five men were standing by a truck. As always, the prisoners clambered aboard; the armed soldiers followed. The tailboard was fastened and the truck left the courtyard.

'Where are we going?' a man with the weather-beaten face of a peasant, asked calmly.

'I don't know.'

'Ruhe!' an SS guard ordered.

A boy, not more than sixteen, began to whimper. The vehicle chugged its way towards Perugia, crossing the bridge over the Chiascio, the bridge over the Tiber, occasionally passing truckloads of soldiers and supplies moving in convoys by the light of hooded sidelights. Suddenly I noticed a military Volkswagen in the distance, moving fast until it caught up with us. Next to the driver I saw the rigid figure of Captain von den Velde. Apparently, I thought, he wanted to witness my execution, or perhaps at the last moment obtain my confession and all the information I could supply. The cold, brisk dawn wind blew into my face from the south, from the direction of Deruta, and I whispered goodbye to my family, for I knew with absolute certainty that, even if I were to confess and tell all, I would still be shot afterwards.

The familiar buildings of Perugia were silent and strange at night with their dark windows. We passed the railway station, then the Piazza IV November and a few other streets before the truck slowed down. Gates opened and were then bolted behind us. We were in the walled-in, strongly lit Carcere Femminile, the former women's prison. The Volkswagen was parked beside us and von den Velde was standing by his car, the white baton in his hand. He barely gave me a glance, but watched the burly German SS sergeant who went from cell to cell accompanied by his guards and called names—one or two from each cell—and then ordered his men to bring the condemned to the back wall, which was topped with a high barbed wire barrier.

A tremor shot through my whole body and my throat tightened with fear. Von den Velde impatiently looked at his watch. It was already past five o'clock. The execution was late. It was not in Ordnung, he told the sergeant. Hastily the German called five names; the prisoners were lined up against the wall and the OVRA men assisted by blindfolding them with black bands. Puffing from exertion, fat Don Giovanni, a breviary in his hand, rushed out of the prison. He halted as he saw me. 'Dio mio!' he said, 'Dio mio!' Then he hurried forward to join the troop of SS men with rifles at the ready being lined up by their sergeant opposite the condemned men. The prison priest began to offer his prayers. I heard a scream piercing the night, 'Long live Italy!' It was the man who had asked me where we were going. Von den Velde raised his baton and flicked it down sharply. A salvo of shots reverberated from the walls of the prison. The five bodies fell to the ground. One of them jerked; the man was still alive. Coolly, the Captain pulled out his revolver and fired. 'Next group!' he said.

My eyes filled with tears. I shut them and began muttering, 'Requiem aeternam dona eis, Domine—Lord, give them eternal rest.' I was uttering prayers for the executed men. But at the same time, I was saying a requiem for myself.

XVII

When I opened my eyes I saw Captain von den Velde facing me.
'Are you ready to confess?'

I drew a shuddering breath. 'I have nothing to confess.'

He waved his baton towards the prison. 'In there!' he ordered. I shuffled across the courtyard with von den Velde close behind.

We entered the building. He pointed to a small room on the right in front of which stood an OVRA man. The Captain entered first and sat behind a small desk, leaving me standing. I was almost fainting from mental and physical exhaustion. 'May I have some water?' I asked.

He ignored my request. 'Get me Giorgio Cianura and Paolo Jozsa!' he shouted to the Italian guard. He drummed his fingers on the desk, waiting. Another burst of gunfire from the courtyard broke the silence. 'You are not afraid of death, Padre?' he asked, almost curiously.

'I am only afraid of God,' I answered evenly.

In the door Giorgio appeared in a drab grey prisoner's uniform. I hardly recognised him. The once rosy, healthy cheeks were hollow; the once bright eyes stared at me in a colourless daze. 'Do you know this man?' the Captain asked me.

'I told you I do. He came to confession.'

Von den Velde sat on the desk near me, in his favourite interrogatory position. 'And what did he confess to? To belonging to the anti-German underground?'

I summoned the little strength and intelligence that I could muster. 'The Catholic confession is privileged. The priest cannot divulge any of it. But that much I can assure you—it contained nothing political.'

Now Paolo Jozsa entered the room; his small body seemed to me to have shrunk even further. At the sight of me he blinked nervously. Von den Velde turned to him. 'Do you know this monk?'

'I saw him in Assisi, I think,' Pali answered.

'Is his name Petar Marinovich?' the SS officer cracked. 'Is this the man who provided you with your documents?' He was having his fun.

'He sometimes came to San Quirico,' Pali mumbled, 'and sometimes offered me a cigarette.'

Von den Velde went on plying us with questions, trying to catch us out, but he was not succeeding. Cavalrymen, I suppose, make poor Gestapo inquisitors, though perhaps they try harder, in order to appear professional. Finally he gave up. 'Back to your cells,' he said to both Pali and Giorgio. 'You come with me, Padre.'

Through the corridor door I could see the dawn light breaking into the prison courtyard. But von den Velde did not lead me back there. He pointed to a cell with a bed, very much like the one I had known for the last three days.

'I am giving you twenty-four hours,' he announced. 'Until dawn tomorrow. Enough time to come to your senses. I am doing it because you are a friend of Colonel Müller's.' I heard the faint tone of mockery in his voice. He walked to the door and turned there. 'And in case you have any suspicion to the contrary, I give you my word as an officer that if you confess and disclose the names of those involved in Assisi's underground you will be released immediately.'

When I awoke a few hours later I saw a nun sitting by my side. She had grey hair and a full, matronly figure. As I opened my eyes, her face broke into a compassionate smile. 'I didn't want to interrupt your sleep,' she said. She pointed to a tray on the small table. There was a glass of milk stand there and a bowl of gruel. 'For you,' she said. 'Please.' I tried to prop myself up on my elbows, but I fell back. With strong arms she helped me up and, all the while holding me, she began feeding me with spoonfuls of warm gruel. My hand attempted to reach for the glass. She handed it to me and I drank the milk all in one go before I let her feed me again. When I had finished eating, she laid me back on the bed and said, 'I think, Padre, you'll probably want to sleep again. You are sleeping badly and need rest.'

'Yes, Sister,' I said faintly. 'Thank you and bless you.' And at once I fell into a deep sleep.

When I awoke again late in the day, it was not the nun, but a man who was sitting on the chair beside me. He had a small, powder-smooth face with an elegantly trimmed moustache. He smiled at me through his pince-nez. Here is another amiable interrogator, I thought. This time from the OVRA.

'I am Avvocato Texeira,' the man said, 'Vincenzo Texeira

from Perugia, and I am your lawyer. I am here to defend you and the other men from Assisi.'

'Oh, since when?'

'Since this morning. My esteemed colleague, Avvocato Fortini, has passed the case on to me.' He shrugged. 'He could not do much and he thought I would do better.'

I managed to sit up in my bed. 'Will you—do better?'

'I hope so. You see, apart from being a good lawyer, I have good connections. As a matter of fact I have already successfully completed the defence of one of the accused. And he is being released immediately.'

'Who?' I asked.

The man laid his hand gently on my arm. 'You, Padre. You are free to go home.'

He helped me to my feet and we walked out, not into the courtyard but out of the front door. An OVRA man checked my release paper, said 'Grazie, Barone' to my companion, and there I was—a free man, on a Perugia street, only hours after my scheduled execution. 'What about the others?' I asked the first question that sprang to my lips.

'Their files', Texeira answered, 'are already on the desk of General Octavius Bube, the German Chief Judge of the Province of Perugia, which means there will be a trial. Or perhaps, if I could prove that the charges are worthless, there won't be any trial at all. I hope I can manage that, at least for some of them. Your file was on the top, by special request of Cardinal della Costa, who phoned Bube himself. The General—he is a very pleasant man, by the way—saw nothing incriminating in your papers, so he ordered your release.'

'And von den Velde agreed?'

Texeira laughed loudly. 'Who is he, a little captain from Bastia?'

'Yes, but an SS captain.'

'That's not as much as being a friend of the Commander-in-Chief of the Wehrmacht in Italy. General Bube happens to be a close and trusted friend of Field-Marshal Kesselring.'

I shook the man's hand in a show of gratitude. 'Then Fortini had the right idea.'

'A very right idea. I have arranged the release of many prisoners through my connections.'

'And who is paying your fee?'

'The Church, of course. Don't worry about that, Padre. I'm sure they'll get my fee for your case from the Order of Frati Minori. You know, there are three things God doesn't know...'

'I know,' I interrupted. 'Where the Franciscans get all their money...'

We broke into a laugh. The air was suddenly filled with the chorus of a black-uniformed band marching through the street, singing 'SS marschiert! Die Strasse frei! Die Sturmkolonnen stehen!' But neither their lusty singing nor the death-heads on their black caps could stop my laughter, not at the old joke, but at a feeling of sheer relief and immeasurable joy at finding myself alive.

As much as I wanted to, I found myself unable to reach the railway station and go straight home. The most I could manage was to get to the Church of San Andrea which had so many times before served me as a place of rest. It was also our Perugia underground headquarters and the relay station between Florence and Assisi. Don Federico Vincenti was just leaving his home to begin vespers when he saw me entering the courtyard. He clapped his hands in delight and surged forward to cradle me in his arms. 'Thank God,' he said, kissing me on my cheek.

I started to tell him about my experience, but I halted almost immediately. 'Let me go with you, Don Federico, and take part in your service.'

He wagged his finger at me. 'Under no circumstances, Padre! You not only look as if you have been exposed to the ordeal of imprisonment and questioning, but also as if you haven't eaten for days.'

'I haven't,' I said. 'But they didn't break me.'

'Go up there,' he said, 'where our refugees are hidden and let Doctor Klugman examine you. You can lie on the bed by the window and hear the service.'

It was no use arguing with him. He was a peasant like me and as strong-willed. I walked up the stairs, from time to time leaning against the banister for support. Then, through a corridor and a narrow door, well camouflaged by a huge religious painting, I made my way into a big hall filled with some thirty people. This was where many of the Perugia Jews lived. They would stop talking the moment the bells rang, for their room was right at the back of the church, and its only window looked down on the people arriving for the service.

When they saw me, many of them rushed forward. Everyone seemed to have been aware that I had been in jail. They had many questions, but Pino Klugman, alias Limani, a tall, spectacled young man, told everyone to be quiet and ordered me to lie down. He had just completed his medical studies at Perugia when the Germans marched in. Once more I did as I was told. He pulled out his stethoscope and listened to my heart and my lungs and then checked my blood pressure. 'You're dehydrated, Padre, that's why your blood pressure is low,' he said. 'You need to drink a lot, but apart from that there is nothing that a good meal won't cure.'

His brother Rico helped me to the window where I lay down on the bed just as I heard the voice of Don Vincenti starting the service. I did not raise my head to look down, since the presence of people upstairs had to be inconspicuous, but I listened and I prayed together with the priest and his congregation. It meant much more to me than my solitary prayers in the Bastia prison cell.

Later in the evening I had my meal. The doctor warned me not to eat too much, but I polished off a nourishing chick-pea soup, a bowl of potatoes and numerous glasses of wine. The doctor's orders were to drink a lot, so I did.

Both my host Don Vincenti and the jovial prison priest Don Giovanni kept me company, the latter drinking almost as much as I to express relief that my life had been spared, and as an escape from the daily strain of administering the last rites to the condemned and attending their execution.

'You were very lucky, Padre Rufino,' he said, twiddling his pudgy thumbs over his large belly, very much like our bishop, 'that Baron Texeira took over your case. And this augurs well for the others too.' He refilled his glass and, pleasantly tipsy and perspiring more than usual, added, 'He has connections.'

'I know. He's a friend of General Bube, the Chief Judge...'

'Not exactly.' The priest's little eyes smiled. 'He has a sister-in-law, Princess Mafalda di Sirignano, a very attractive brunette from Naples—coal-black, beautiful eyes and pleasantly plumpish, just in the right places...'

'Yes,' I said impatiently. 'And?'

'And *she* is the friend of General Bube.' The priest burst out laughing. 'A very intimate friend. *She* is the connection.'

'Thank God,' I uttered, surprising myself with the exclamation. God has his own ways of helping people and who were we to question Him?

'Therefore,' Don Giovanni went on, 'I'm very optimistic about the outcome. This Bube—and mind you, he is a very nice man, though a Protestant—happens to be taken with her looks and her title.'

'But until he intervenes', I said soberly, 'how are we going to protect our men from that Nazi sergeant's daily selection of victims?'

Don Giovanni nodded, as if expecting the question. 'Money,' he said. 'Presents, things of value. The sergeant appreciates gifts.'

'I'll make it my first business of the day to seek help, either from the relatives of the men or from the Bishop.'

'Send everything to me. I'll see to it that the Nazi bastard gets it.'

'I've prepared your bed,' Don Vincenti interrupted. 'I think, Padre Rufino, that you need a good rest.'

'I won't deny it. But meanwhile, Don Giovanni, tell the man...'

'I will tell him', Don Giovanni interrupted, rolling his eyes, 'that the money is coming.'

In Assisi, the Bishop, to whom I went first to offer my thanks, embraced me with 'Figlio mio!' and kissed both my cheeks like a general decorating a soldier. Mother Giuseppina clapped her hands, exclaiming 'Padre, I instructed my sisters to pray for you every day.' She raised her eyes to heaven. 'Thank you, St Clare!' I'm sure that, reserved as she usually was, Mother Giuseppina would have thrown her arms around me if the cloister's grille had not stood between us. And at San Damiano a Catholic mass of thanksgiving and Jewish prayers praising the Lord greeted my arrival.

But throughout my homecoming the fate of our men in Perugia never left my mind. I got two gold sovereigns from Giorgio's parents, now hiding in the grounds of the Bishop's Palace; Pali's fiancée helped me to find the envelope containing fifty American dollars, hidden in the garden of San Quirico; and finally, at my monastery, Professor Fano handed over to me a sizeable amount of Italian money. Two hours after my arrival at Assisi, Franca Covarelli was on her way to Perugia carrying the gifts for the German sergeant.

But before I could relax, I still had to make sure that no one else had been arrested. I found Don Brunacci at the Laboratorio di San Francesco, where he used both to celebrate mass and run his clandestine school for Jewish youngsters. When I arrived there, the children were already gathering. The canon shook my hand warmly, then informed me that, although nobody had been arrested, our underground informants had reported that the town was now teeming with OVRA agents. Von den Velde did not give up; he was searching for hard evidence. Our enemies, Don Aldo said, were equipped with cameras with telephoto lenses. The best I could do was to stay away from the city, at least for a while. And then he proudly pointed at the youngsters in the adjacent room. 'You know, ours is the only school still functioning in Assisi. All the regular school buildings have been requisitioned by Colonel Müller and turned into hospitals. With the Allied offensive now in progress, scores of wounded are arriving daily.'

'The Colonel...' I said. 'He hasn't lifted a finger to help me.'

'Neither is he helping anyone else. He no longer takes his strolls through town, nor attends mass.'

'He has changed.'

'I simply suspect', Don Aldo said, 'that he is being watched and spied upon. And he knows it. And so he is being extra careful, just as I am, just as you will have to be from now on.' He wagged his finger at me in solemn admonition. Then he went to the door.

'Come children, let's begin the lesson.'

XVIII

I did obey the canon's orders. After all, he was my superior. He was in charge of all the refugees; I was only in charge of the Jewish ones. I stayed at San Damiano, minding my own affairs, except for seeing to it that occasionally the sergeant got more gift parcels. We had now resorted to a collection; Texeira and the princess and the general were certainly taking their time. So some of the others chipped in and Nino Maionica, in particular, gave us gold before he went into the mountains to join the guerilla band led by the two Americans. But as a result our men in Perugia were safe for the time being. Apparently touched by our last generous gift, the Nazi sergeant even allowed Lea Romeo, formerly Hella Gelb, to see her fiancé.

And then one day, in the second half of April, when I had finished my mass and was ready to take a walk and enjoy the wonderful weather and the sight of my brothers tilling the soil, I saw a military Volkswagen drive into our courtyard. I felt a sharp stab of fear, thinking that once more von den Velde had come to claim me. I summoned all my courage and went up to the car. I could hardly believe my eyes. It was Giorgio Kropf, in civilian clothes, with a German armband, reading 'Dolmetscher.' There was no one else in the car. 'Giorgio!' I clapped my hands. 'My God! Did you escape?' It was the first thought that came to my mind.

He broke into a chuckle, 'I was released, Padre.' And he embraced me. He still looked ill, but no longer so deathly pale.

'Released?' The German military vehicle, the armband were confusing me. 'And the others?'

'Pali, Bruno and Finzi were also set free. Gay and Podda, I'm afraid not. Not yet, anyway.'

As usual, some of my brothers were behind me in the church doorway. But there were no Jews around, not even the maestro di musica to learn about his son's release.

'Was there a trial?'

'No trial. General Bube reached the conclusion that both mine and Bruno's papers were in perfect order and that there was no reason to keep us in jail. Pali, admittedly, had acquired documents of a deceased person, claiming he had lost his own in the war. He had partially paid for it with two months in jail, but he would probably have been sentenced to a year or two if not for the Führer's help.' I shook my head, perplexed. 'You see,' Giorgio went on, enjoying the suspense of his dramatic account, 'Adolf Hitler was fifty-five on 20 April. In honour of his birthday, the Chief Judge of the Province of Perugia decided that there ought to be an amnesty for a number of Italian prisoners, who had either served light sentences or were facing minor charges. Pali belonged to the latter category.'

'But, what does this military car, this German sign on your arm mean?'

'It means that I am employed by the Wehrmacht.'

'How, for God's sake?'

'My cousin, Princess Mafalda di Sirignano...'

'Giorgio, stop it!'

'Well...' Giorgio took out a packet of cigarettes. 'Try them, Padre. They are good. German.' He lit one for me and then one for himself. 'I have never met as smart a lawyer as this Texeira. A few days after you were released, I was told that a visitor was waiting for me in the prison office. Then, with Armando Rocchi watching, this beautiful girl threw her arms around me and cried, "My poor Giorgio, my dearest cousin!" Obviously, the Italian prefect and chief of police of Perugia could not refuse the German Chief Judge's decision to dismiss charges against me. And then, as I told you, Hitler's birthday came just in time for Pali. And naturally, as the General tried to be very helpful to his sweetheart's beloved cousin, he found me employment as an interpreter with the Department of Agriculture of the Military Command of the Province of Perugia. And because Pali was almost my brother-in-law, he found a similar job for him in his own office. Don't forget Pali had a German mother and I was born in Vienna. We both speak perfect German; we are of great value to the Army of the Third Reich.'

Slowly my face lightened and I broke into laughter. Giorgio laughed with me, lustily. 'But tell me,' I asked, 'why is it that if you are a cousin of the princess, Bube employed Pali instead of you?'

Giorgio smiled his lively, open smile. 'Well, perhaps because General Bube was not entirely sure of a handsome Italian, half his age, even though he was the cousin of his girl-friend. So it was safer to put me elsewhere. She is a very attractive girl, this Mafalda, I must admit. You see, it runs in the family!'

I accompanied Giorgio back to his car. Except for his looks, he really was his old self, oozing confidence. With a great deal of satisfaction he showed me his official pass, signed by some Sonderführer on behalf of the Militaerkommandantur 1018, asking all to assist Giorgio Cianura, in the employ of the German Army, in the execution of his duties. 'Obviously, Padre, Pali and I could be of great help to all of us here,' he said. He started his motor, then impulsively leaned out of the window and embraced me. 'See you soon, Padre.'

On 11 May 1944, the attack on Monte Cassino began. If it fell, the road to Rome and beyond would be open. And with the Allied offensive in full swing the guerilla bands started to be extremely active, ambushing German military convoys almost daily. It was von den Velde's job to secure the safety of the Wehrmacht troops in our area. And both SS and OVRA men began making numerous arrests of people suspected of helping the partisans. On 15 May Don Brunacci was put under OVRA escort and taken to Perugia. I could only guess at the ordeal that the canon was subjected to and my only consolation was the knowledge that once more the Bishop would do all in his power to help secure Brunacci's release. It was three days later, in the morning, just after we heard on the radio that Monte Cassino had fallen and that the march on Rome had begun, that the young sacristan of Santa Maria Maggiore came to San Damiano to fetch me.

I immediately hurried to the town. Nicolini knew that I ought to stay away, so, since he asked me to risk this trip, he must have an urgent task for me. There he sat in his library, impatiently twiddling his thumbs. 'Sorry, Padre,' he said waving away the ceremony of obeisance, 'but we must act immediately. Until today not one Jew has been arrested. But last night, a boy by the name of David Levi, aged sixteen or seventeen, who lives in my grounds, was caught after curfew. Our informer has just reported to me that the police have found out that the boy is a Jew. We must stop them at any cost from handing him over to the Gestapo.'

'Why was he out during curfew?' I asked.

The Bishop threw up his hands. 'Youth!' he said. 'Love! He has an Italian girl-friend.'

'Did he confess to being Jewish?' Involuntarily my eyes darted to the door as if expecting the Gestapo to burst through it at any moment.

'He didn't have to. The chief of police, Bertolucci, is from Naples and he recognised the boy. His father was a tailor there and, as luck would have it, made a police uniform for Bertolucci when he served in the Naples police.'

I rubbed my face. My God, we'd managed so far, but now with one stroke of fate all might be lost. 'I'll go there right away.'

'You must,' the Bishop said. 'I don't know what you can do, but you must!'

I rushed out of the Palace. Fifteen minutes later I reached the police headquarters on the Via Fontebella and at once asked to see the chief of police. I was ushered into his office. There he sat, fat from years of consuming pasta, his pomaded hair parted in the middle. 'Padre, it's not the matter of the arrest of one of your Catholic refugees. We have caught a Jew, and strongly suspect that among those refugees there may be dozens of them, to say the least.' He offered me a cigarette, a gesture acquired from his Nazi superiors, but I brushed it aside.

'What do you plan to do with the boy?'

'I have already issued orders to hand him over to Captain von den Velde. I'm sure he will want to question him personally.' The man's thick lips parted in a self-satisfied smile, as if he expected my congratulations.

'Rescind the order,' I said.

'Don't be silly, Padre.'

'Release the boy,' I said adamantly. He just laughed in response. 'Listen, Bertolucci.' I moved my chair towards his. 'You heard the news on the radio?'

'No, what has happened?'

'Monte Cassino fell today, the Gustav Line has been broken,

and the Allies are advancing towards Rome. They will be in Assisi in a few weeks. The Russians are moving forward, the Allies will land in Europe any day now. The war is coming to an end.'

'What has that to do with the case?'

'It has a lot to do with the case—with your case. You have been in the service of the Fascists and the Nazis for years now. With this one good action you can redeem yourself. It's time to think of your own future, Bertolucci, and I am speaking to you not only as a priest, threatening you with God's punishment for the boy's execution. You ought to consider your future not only in heaven, but also on earth. I'll be the first to stand up for you if you only save the boy.'

The police chief squinted at me, then got up from his chair and walked over to the window. It was several minutes before he finally turned. His eyes were solemn now, focusing on my face. The moment he slumped back heavily into his chair, I knew I had won. He picked up the phone, mentioned the name of a police sergeant, then said, 'This boy we arrested last night—release him.'

His change of heart was no surprise to me. I had no doubt that many Italian Fascists after the war would claim loudly that they had always supported the Allies.

He accompanied me to the door, with his arm around my shoulders. 'By the way,' he said, 'I've just learned that Don Brunacci has been released—on condition that he be sent to the Vatican.' Whatever he knew, and I bet he knew plenty, he did not say. He did not say one word.

Two weeks later my foe turned friend, Police Chief Bertolucci, informed me that a company of Wehrmacht sappers had arrived in Assisi and had begun to plant mines under the most important public buildings. The Germans were determined to leave the city in ruins. And the news seemed the more bitter because only the day before our Bishop had received the order, signed by the Allied Commander, General Alexander, and transmitted through the good offices of the Vatican, that his forces would treat Assisi with the respect due to its holy character and avoid bombarding and shelling it. Fortini's efforts had been successful, Müller's had not. Unless both sides agreed, Assisi was destined to become a heap of ruins.

Again I abandoned the relative safety of San Damiano and made my way to Assisi, anxious to see whether the Germans were mining our basilicas as well. I saw the sappers, guarded by helmeted SS soldiers, their guns at the ready, putting explosives under the Casa del Comune and the Palace of the Captain of the People, then moving on towards the Piazza di San Francesco. A crowd of inhabitants, many of them monks and priests, kept at a distance by the German troops, followed the sappers. I ran round through the Via San Paolo and reached the Basilica before them.

'Where is Padre Todde?' I cried to a group of monks standing in front of the building.

'He dashed over to see the Bishop,' one of them answered. 'Look, Padre!' And he pointed to the white and yellow flag of the Vatican flying over the Basilica. I sighed, doubting whether it would stop the Germans. Impulsively, I started to rush towards the Hotel Subasio, wondering whether my intervention would do any good, not even certain that the Colonel would receive me. But then had he not, for months, prayed daily at the Basilica, lying prostrate in front of the Holy Saint's grave? Which claimed his ultimate allegiance, the Catholic Church or Germany? And if he was afraid, so was I. Was it not more important, even in times of greatest danger, to stand up for your God rather than your country? When I had almost reached the hotel, I looked back. The soldiers were nowhere in sight. Perhaps they had stopped at some other buildings. Perhaps they had never intended to mine the basilicas, since this single act would antagonise their Italian ally.

I saw a German military vehicle halt in front of the hotel entrance. I walked past it but a call of 'Padre Rufino!' brought me to a stop. I looked back. Paolo Jozsa was getting out of the car. I had seen Giorgio often in the past weeks; he had several times asked me to notify some peasant family that his outfit would come to confiscate their cows or horses and that they should hide their animals in the forest. But I had not seen Pali since the day of our confrontation in Perugia prison. He had also recovered and looked well-nourished, though his usual nervousness was visible in his face. 'What are you doing here?' I asked.

'This!' He showed me a document. 'Delivering it to Colonel Müller.'

I looked at it, but except for the date, 31 May 1944, the signature of Field-Marshal Albert Kesselring and an official stamp, I could not make it out. 'I don't read German', I said.

'It's the recognition by the Commander of the Wehrmacht in Italy of Assisi's status as an open city.'

'What?' I almost screamed. My eyes turned to the sky and I clapped my hands with delight. 'Grazie a Dio!' I uttered. 'Thank God!'

'I'll be right back!' Paolo said, and I saw him disappear through the door. I did not follow him; I waited, pacing up and down the pavement. It was five minutes later that Pali returned. I noticed the same 'Dolmetscher' band on his arm as Giorgio's. His face was now all smiles. 'Orders have already been issued', he said, 'to halt the sappers, to dismantle the mines, and to get the SS troops out of town.'

I embraced Pali with such a force as if it were he and not Field-Marshal Kesselring who had issued the order. The young man opened the door of his car. 'How is it that you are delivering the order?' I asked.

'It came to our headquarters this morning,' he answered, 'and I volunteered to deliver it, since I knew, and General Bube knew, that the public buildings of Assisi were already being mined.'

'The Pope has done a splendid job,' I said.

Pali was about to start his car. 'The Pope?' he grinned, leaning confidentially towards me. His voice sank to a whisper. 'No, the Jewish refugee in the employ of the Wehrmacht, repaying his debt to the city that has saved him.'

I blinked. 'What do you mean? For God's sake, Pali, what do you mean?'

'I mean that the trusted friend of Field-Marshal Kesselring had in his office official blank papers, signed and stamped by the Field-Marshal in case of an emergency. All *I* had to do was to fill in the blank space.' He smiled. 'You think I haven't learned a thing or two from Luigi Brizi? But—and he placed a finger on his lips—'stai zitto, Padre—not a word to anyone!' And before I could say Pater Noster he was gone, leaving me behind, no longer serene and confident. This had been a daring forgery, too daring for my comfort. Pali was taking on not only the Colonel but also his staff and, most of all, von den Velde. If the ruse were discovered, we would all be put against the wall and shot—just a week or two before our liberation.

I started to walk away when another army vehicle stopped in front of the hotel and I recognised Colonel Müller's car. He himself was coming through the door, accompanied by two of his aides. 'Padre!' he shouted. I turned. 'Look!' He was waving the document I had seen a moment ago. 'Come, come with us! we're going to the Bishop, to inform him officially.'

'Officially, of what?' I asked, feigning ignorance.

'Assisi has been proclaimed an open city!' I came forward, smiling. 'Isn't that wonderful?' The Colonel shook both my hands as if he had seen me only yesterday and not two months ago. 'Get in, Padre!' He pushed me into the car next to his two officers and got into the front seat beside the driver. 'Thank God my letter to Kesselring has had its effect. And just in time!'

Giuseppe Placido Nicolini, the Bishop of Assisi, was waiting for us in his library. Stunned by the arrival of the three German officers, his little eyes searched mine as I appeared behind the Germans. He knew all about the German sappers from Padre Todde, who was standing by his side. When the Colonel said in Italian that he had official and important news to communicate, and looked hesitantly at the library bookshelves, Padre Todde quickly suggested that we move to the reception room, so that the Bishop could receive his visitors more properly. But Nicolini waved his hand. 'Let's not stand on ceremony. What is it, Colonello?'

Müller cleared his throat, then he and his aides drew themselves up. Standing there very stiff, very German, in a formal voice the Colonel said, 'I have the honour to inform Your Excellency that Field-Marshal Albert Kesselring, Wehrmacht Commander-in-Chief, Southern Command, has declared Assisi an open city.' He paused for a moment and when he saw the solemn, frightened face of the Bishop break into a huge smile he continued. 'I have already dispatched my other aides to order the sappers to dismantle the mines and ask the SS troops to leave the city.' At that moment, our little Bishop rushed forward and put his arms around the tall Colonel. Then, from sheer joy, he embraced the two other bewildered officers of the Wehrmacht. He clapped his hands loudly to bring his niece, and when Emilia appeared at the door he shouted, 'Get that last bottle of Santa Giustina and six glasses. Quick!'

We all now relaxed, sat down and chatted happily. The wine was brought in, the bottle already uncorked. The glasses were filled by the Bishop himself, then he raised his. 'To you, Colonel, with a million thanks.'

'To Field-Marshal Kesselring,' Colonel Müller said. 'He deserves the thanks.'

We toasted the Field-Marshal, in a happy, comradely mood. Then one of the Colonel's aides said, after taking a sip, 'Not bad, not bad at all. It's almost as good as our Moselle.' This was the highest tribute a German officer could pay to Italian wine.

Colonel Müller got up. 'We had better go. I want to verify personally that my orders are being carried out.' For a moment I thought that he would kneel down to make his Catholic obeisance, but he caught himself in time, glanced uncomfortably at his officers, and saluted the Bishop.

'May we go with you?' I asked, eager to witness the departure of German troops from Assisi. Padre Todde kissed the Bishop's ring, and Nicolini blessed us with the sign of the cross.

The very moment we crossed the gate, I saw the familiar Volkswagen coming to a halt and Captain von den Velde storming out of it. He rushed forward and saluted the Colonel. The two men engaged in a brisk and rough German conversation which Padre Todde later translated for my benefit.

'I was told you had gone to the Bishop, Colonel,' von den Velde said, 'so I rushed here. One of your officers informed me that you had ordered my men out of the city.'

'That is right,' Colonel Müller said. He pulled out the document. 'Here, read it for yourself.'

I watched von den Velde's eyes squinting, scrutinising the paper, and my heart stopped. After a while he raised his head. 'There are two thousand German soldiers in the town,' he said.

'That's right. Two thousand wounded soldiers under my care. Their evacuation begins tomorrow.'

'With all due respect, Colonel,' the SS captain said angrily, raising his voice, 'I am responsible for their safety. I am responsible for security in Assisi.'

'And I am responsible for Assisi,' Colonel Müller answered stiffly. Then he added. 'A company of regular troops will remain until the evacuation is completed. But I want all SS troops to leave at once, and I'm going to see to it, personally, that all your men are out of here within an hour.'

I watched von den Velde—the internal struggle reflected in his face, the nervous tic contorting his mouth. He finally took hold of himself and raised his hand in salute. 'Jawohl, Herr Stadtkommissar,' he said and stalked back to his car. I watched his Volkswagen leave the Piazza del Vescovado, never to return to Assisi again, and I only wished I had the rank of our Lord Bishop so that I, too, could take Colonel Müller into my grateful arms.

XIX

On 4 June 1944, Rome was liberated and two days later the Allied armies landed in northern France. Kesselring and his staff retreated to Foligno, but it was obviously a temporary move. There was nothing to stop the Allied advance until they reached the strongly fortified Gothic Line running along the river Foglia, well north of Assisi. From San Damiano I could hear, day and night, the steady roar of vehicles moving along the highway, away from the front. Occasionally my brothers and I would walk to the main road, to watch the tanks, the truck-loads of troops and supplies, and the columns of German soldiers marching out of step, exhausted, dirty and half starved.

One day, the representative of the Military Command 1018, Department of Agriculture, Giorgio Cianura, arrived, drove to the Via Portico and presented an official authorisation to the German warehouse to distribute flour, oil and sugar immediately to the starved population of Assisi. Having done this and observed that the order was carried out, he drove to my monastery.

'Padre,' he said hastily, when I came out to see him in his car. His eyes glistened strangely. 'You have an informer in Bastia. Get me some information about von den Velde's movements. Müller chased him out of town, but not out of Santa Maria degli Angeli. He has had the station and the flour mill there mined; the explosives are ready to be set off the day the Germans leave. Let your man tell us when von den Velde is about to drive to the village.'

'I don't understand what for? And who are "we"?'

'The partisans. Pali and I have been working with them. We want to ambush his car. It's not just in revenge for what he has done to us. The bastard bragged to me during the interrogation that he personally has killed forty-two Jews and anti-Fascists.'

I pondered for a second. 'No, Giorgio,' I said. 'We, priests and monks, are here to save people's lives, not to take them.'

'What?' Giorgio grew visibly annoyed. 'You suffered at his hands as much as we did.' There was a fanaticism in his eyes that I had not noticed before.

'What you do is your business,' I said, 'but don't count on me to help you. I won't be the judge of who is to die. God created life, let Him decide when it should end.'

Giorgio tightened his lips angrily and started his car. He leaned out. 'Padre, I am a Jew and you know what the Nazis have done to us. Can you understand?'

'I do, Giorgio. And I am a priest. Can *you* understand?'

'They have killed more than three thousand priests in Europe!' Giorgio retorted. And he drove off fast, shaking his head, not understanding at all.

It was impossible to see Colonel Müller. Twenty-four hours a day he and his staff were seeing to the evacuation of the wounded. Many of them had to be taken by ambulance to the railway station of Santa Maria degli Angeli. The inhabitants of Assisi occasionally caught a glimpse of the Colonel either in his car or on foot, rushing from one hospital to another. And only when a handful of the wounded remained did they see the Wehrmacht company clamber on to their trucks and drive off. The Colonel was not afraid to remain in the city. The Italian partisans had passed word to him that not a hair of his head would be touched.

I remember that day distinctly—16 June. The rumble of trucks along the main highway had almost ceased, and I walked to the town, knowing that it would not be long now before the last German left. I had to go to say goodbye to that German.

When I reached the Porta Nuova, I saw the entrance to the city blocked by two crossed wooden boards, painted white and red. The barricade was manned by a few young men. 'Hey, Padre!' the leader of the group called. I turned and saw—Paolo Jozsa. But this time he was not wearing his 'Dolmetscher' armband. Instead, like the other men, he wore a white armband, featuring a big red cross. 'We are representatives of the International Red Cross,' he said, 'observing the parties' respect for Assisi's status as an open city.'

I now recognised the others—there was Trento Brizi and Nino Maionica, who had come down from the mountains, and Bruno Fano. 'All the seven gates to the city are barricaded,' Pali went on, importantly. 'We are seeing to it that no German troops return. We've ordered the sappers to dismantle the explosives set under the flourmill, the Montecatini Chemical works and the railway station.' From his pocket he pulled a document. 'Do you want to see my official nomination from the Geneva headquarters of the International Red Cross?'

I waved the paper away. I knew very well that it came from the same office as the German approval of Assisi's status as an open city and Giorgio's order to distribute food. Pali grinned boyishly at me and grandly waved me into the city.

Half a kilometre further on I saw Giorgio Cianura, another former Dolmetscher, now also wearing the white band with a red cross. He sat in his Volkswagen, but the German military car now had a huge red cross painted over its doors. 'Requisitioned!' Giorgio shouted to me. Beside him sat the young

David Levi, the boy I had helped to release from jail. 'We are patrolling the town,' Giorgio informed me.

The Piazza del Comune was unusually quiet, even though it was a beautiful day. Except for the patrolling Red Cross 'officials', the town was quiet, as though people were holding their breath, uncertain what the last hours of occupation would bring.

I went to the hospitals and the schools turned into hospitals. There was no one there, but beds, medical equipment and glass cabinets filled with medicine had been left intact. Finally I found the Colonel in the House for the Blind and Deaf-Mutes, where there were still a dozen or so German soldiers lying in their beds, awaiting transport. When Müller saw me in the door, he hurried forward with a salute and an embrace. 'I'm so glad you came, Padre. I just telephoned the Bishop and he's expecting me. Will you come along?' He guided me to the exit. 'I was going to come to San Damiano to say goodbye to you. Oh, Hauptmann Knabbe!' He turned to an officer just entering the room and gave his orders.

'Jawohl, Herr Oberst,' the captain answered.

'I told him,' Müller explained to me on the way out, 'to complete the evacuation and to accompany that last group on the train.'

The car was waiting in front of the building. 'The Bishop's Palace,' Müller said, and ushered me into the back seat while he settled himself as usual in front, beside his driver.

This time the Lord Bishop received the Colonel in his reception hall, sitting on his throne, wearing a black cassock edged with red, a purple zucchetto and the golden pectoral cross. After all, it was a farewell ceremony; the military commander was leaving the city. Colonel Müller, his hat in hand, approached the throne and went down on one knee. Reverently, his lips touched the episcopal ring. Nicolini stretched out a hand and raised him to his feet. As I in turn made my obeisance, the Bishop joked, 'Are you leaving, too, Padre?' He spoke without a smile, he just wanted to ease the tension.

He gestured to Müller to sit down. 'We shall miss you, Colonel,' he said. 'I wish I had something to offer you to remember us by.' Searchingly, he looked around the hall.

'I don't even have any good wine left. We drank the last bottle together two weeks ago.'

'I shall always remember the taste,' Müller said, 'because of the occasion. However, Your Excellency, I have something to offer you. I will be honoured if you accept my modest gift for Assisi.'

'What is that?'

'I have issued orders not to empty our warehouse at Via Portico. Apart from food, there are large quantities of medical supplies, surgical instruments, physiotherapy equipment, and enough medicine to last for a long time. And of course nothing was moved from our hospitals, except'—he smiled—'the people.'

I opened my mouth and gaped at Nicolini. He was speechless. 'It is worth a fortune!' the Bishop finally uttered.

'The official estimate is 100 million lire,' Müller said simply.

I gulped hard. A city clerk made 3,000 lire a month.

'I don't know how to thank you,' Nicolini said. 'We shall never forget that you saved Assisi from destruction, and now this generous gift... I'm overwhelmed. Thank you, thank you for everything!' He opened his arms to the man.

'And we thank St Francis for sending the Colonello to us,' I added, unsolicited, while the Bishop was bestowing kisses on the German officer's cheeks.

Colonel Müller kissed the ring, then got up, slightly embarrassed by the Bishop's outburst of gratitude. Obviously he wanted no thanks. 'Come, Padre,' he said to me. 'If you're going home, I'll take you there.'

'Oh, that's all right, Colonel. I can walk. You must be in a hurry.'

'Oh, I have time. But let's stop for a minute at the hospital. I must check if my orders have been carried out.'

A few minutes later, when we approached the building, I saw several ambulances in front. Orderlies were carrying a wounded German paratrooper to a vehicle. 'The last man,' one of them said. Captain Knabbe came out of the building and, when he saw the Colonel, saluted and reported that the evacuation was complete. He asked his superior a question, but Müller waved him on. Apparently he told the officer not to wait for him;

he would leave later. The Captain saluted again, then raised his hand. 'Heil Hitler!' he said.

'Grüss Gott,' Colonel Müller answered.

As we drove through the city, he looked out of the car window, as if trying to remember the cobbled streets, the archways, the pots of geraniums hanging from the balconies. At the Porta Nuova our vehicle was halted. Pali came forward, saw us, saluted first the Colonel, then me, and quickly ordered the barricade to be moved. We crossed the empty highway, and then drove down the path.

The car came to a stop in our courtyard. I opened the door. It was time to say goodbye and it was not easy, but fortunately Colonel Müller stepped out of the car, too. Without a word, he walked into St Francis's Church. I remained in the entrance. He was alone in the church where once I had heard his confession and given him absolution. I watched him light a candle, kneel in front of the crucifix and bury his face in his hands. After a few minutes he rose to his feet and when he came back to the door he noticed a throng of friars assembled behind him, all eager to wish him Godspeed. Seeing how moved he was, I waved my hands exuberantly. 'We don't have Moselle or Santa Giustina, Colonel, but could we toast you with an Umbrian country wine?'

He was only too eager to accept and to let me lead him to our refectory, sit him down on a bench and order the wine. He watched the monks assemble in the room, all of them. As numerous glasses were being filled, Maestro Fano in his brown habit, with his huge mop of white hair protruding from under his zucchetto, sat at a small organ in the corner of the room. 'I want to play something for you, Colonello,' he said. He pressed his fingers on the keys. It was not a Gregorian chant, but another lovely religious melody. 'I composed the music', he said proudly, 'for St Francis's "Canticle of the Creatures".'

We listened for a while as he himself recited the verse to the music. I looked at Müller and he looked back at me. We both remembered how he had discovered the words chiselled in stone in St Clare's Garden. He leaned towards me. 'Padre Rufino,' he said, 'I do hope you'll forgive me the intrusion into your monastery and my unjust suspicions. That SS captain really made me believe that you were hiding people wanted by our authorities.'

Magnanimously, I raised my glass. 'You are forgiven, Colonel.'

His face relaxed and he turned to all in the room. 'Imagine, that silly young fool insisting that your poor Padre Rufino was the head of Assisi's vast underground organisation.' He burst out laughing, and we all joined in. 'Cin cin!' he said, getting up and raising his glass to me and then to all of us. And everyone in the room, all the Christian and Jewish friars, toasted him with their wine.

I accompanied the Colonel to his car. The crimson light of sunset began to flicker through the leaves of evergreens and olive trees. 'Will you come back—after the war?' I asked.

'Of course. And I'll bring my family along—my wife and my children.'

'You'll be most welcome, Colonello.'

'I must collect my belongings from the hotel and then I will take my last stroll through the city. I haven't had a chance to do so for a long time, and the town is at its loveliest at this hour. I have said my goodbyes to you and the Bishop and now I must bid my farewell to Assisi.'

XX

At dawn the next day we were awakened by a deafening rumble. Partially dressed, barefoot, girding our habits on our way, we all ran to the highway. There, from the south, from the direction of Foligno, tanks were roaring forward, helmeted heads peering out of the open turret hatches. Across the road a crowd gathered, young girls holding carafes of wine and glasses, children waving bouquets of wild flowers. When the first tank had reached us, we began to wave happily and applaud and cry, 'Vivan i nostri liberatori!'

From his turret the commanding officer leaned out. 'Are there any Jerries left in town?' he yelled as loud as he could, to overcome both the noise of his machines and our welcome.

'No!' Fra Euralio, who spoke English, shouted back. 'They've all gone!' The officer raised his hand to motion a right turn into the direction of the Porta Nuova. But suddenly, as he was manoeuvring his tank, he saw, we all saw, a little boy running down the road towards the vehicle, frantically waving his hands, almost falling under its tracks. Abruptly the tank came to a halt. It was Pio Caianella.

'What does he want?' the officer cried to Fra Euralio.

The boy turned to the monk and began talking, animatedly, pointing towards Santa Maria degli Angeli and making circular movements with his arm. The friar translated what the boy wanted. Pio, the ten- or eleven-year-old resistance fighter, was suggesting that the British armoured column continue straight ahead, then turn into a side mountain road and come down again behind the river Chiascio, cutting off the German garrison in Bastia.

'There is an entire SS battalion there!' the boy explained feverishly. 'If you take them by surprise and blow up the bridge across the river, you'll trap them all, without a fight.'

The officer in command was a handsome lieutenant with a small moustache. His eyes beamed as he pursed his lips and yelled 'Straight on!' to the column. Then he said to Pio, 'Jump in and show us the way.' The British lieutenant leaned out, stretched his arms, grabbed the boy, and lifted him all the way up to the turret opening, then he shoved him inside the tank, next to himself. We stood there, watching the vehicle start off again, followed by other tanks, then by a long line of armoured cars, then truck-loads of infantrymen, helmets tipped over their noses, guns slung across their backs, waving off the wine and flowers, motioning that they would be back, too busy with their next assignment to stop even for a moment. Not a single Allied vehicle had entered the city.

We ran alongside the column, deciding to go to the Basilica of Santa Maria degli Angeli and to wait there. In front of the Basilica stood Father Sebastian and his brothers, waving to the soldiers, and from across the street the villagers shouted their joy, not understanding why the Allied soldiers were bypassing Assisi.

The tanks, the armoured cars, the trucks, all disappeared from view, while we waited to hear gunfire from the direction of Bastia. About half an hour later a roaring explosion shattered the windows in many houses. 'They have blown up the bridge over the Chiascio!' I yelled happily, while men and women looked at me, annoyed, inspecting the damage done to their homes.

'Come,' Father Sebastian said. 'It's time for lauds.' It was the same hour of the day when I had started my first mission nine months earlier, in September 1943, and the same place, the Basilica of Santa Maria degli Angeli. In all that time not a single person to whom we had offered asylum had been deported or killed by the Nazis.

The bells rang for the service, then stopped, then rang again. Impulsively, I started to count—yes, they rang five times, then after a pause they rang five times again. Then I burst out laughing. It was Father Sebastian's joke. It was good to joke now, with no more real danger facing us. I watched the service conducted in the Chapel of the Transition, suddenly recalling how the Basilica had acquired its name. The legend had it, that in medieval times pilgrims heard angels sing at the holy ground where St Francis had died. On that early morning of 17 June 1944, when Assisi was about to be liberated, I too thought that I could hear the angels singing.

No gunfire was heard from the direction of Bastia. And two hours later we saw a tank, two armoured cars and several truckloads of soldiers coming back. The rest of the column had apparently moved forward, towards Perugia.

When the tank came closer, we saw the British lieutenant and Pio Caianella beaming next to him. 'Here, Padre,' the officer shouted to Fra Euralio. He lifted the boy up high and then let him slide down the tank into the friar's arms. 'Here is your little hero. He ought to get a medal!'

Excitedly, Pio started to relate what had happened in Bastia, but the British officer interrupted him, saying something to Fra Euralio, then waiting for him to announce what he had said. 'The British commander said', Father Euralio shouted aloud, so that all of us on the street could hear him, 'that they are only going to pass through the town to flush out possible snipers.'

The commander turned his tank in the direction of the Porta Nuova and the armoured cars followed. From all over the town and the neighbouring villages came the joyful ringing of bells. Finally, after a little delay, the British were entering Assisi.

As the trucks passed us, a few of my brothers and I jumped on to them, helped up by the soldiers. And of course Pio was with us, continuing his story. 'How about the commander of that battalion?' I asked anxiously. 'Has he been caught?'

'That captain with the white baton?' Pio asked knowingly. 'Of course, no one managed to escape. The entire SS battalion surrendered without firing a single shot.' There, I thought, justice has been done, and I was glad I had not helped Giorgio in his plan.

All the way towards the Basilica of St Francis, the narrow old streets of Assisi were lined with inhabitants and Catholic and Jewish refugees, who all came streaming out to welcome the Allies. And those who were not on the street crowded the balconies and the windows of the houses flanking the road. This time the grateful soldiers accepted wine and kissed signorine in turn, and some of the girls had already found their way on to the trucks, settling themselves beside us on the laps of the British soldiers. In front of the column the lieutenant rode in his open tank, several garlands of flowers hanging around his neck. As we came through the Via Frate Elia into the Piazza di San Francesco, I saw the police band awaiting us. The moment the British column appeared in sight, the band struck up a march of welcome. The tank halted and all the other vehicles stopped in the piazza. The Lieutenant jumped to the ground.

Immediately, the police commander approached him and saluted. Bertolucci was delivering the city to the Allies, declaring that its inhabitants were grateful for their liberation from the yoke of the German and Fascist occupation. There was enormous applause. People came pouring into the piazza from all the streets leading to it. The officer raised his hand; he wanted to say something, and the crowd fell silent.

'I'm Lieutenant Phillip Garigue,' he shouted as loud as

possible. 'And I am your new military commander. Not for long probably, since I will be replaced by a high-ranking officer. But meanwhile I want to pass on to you the order of the Allied Commander-in-Chief, General Sir Harold Alexander, that the city will continue to be a hospital and convalescent centre, this time for *our* soldiers. No military installations will be set up in town and its holy character will be fully respected.'

He did not finish. The enormous crowd, as big as that usually gathered for the Feast of St Francis, broke into applause. Then I saw some happy faces in that crowd—those of Pali and Giorgio and their fiancées. All four were elbowing their way towards me. Deborah fell into my arms first, tears rolling down her red cheeks. As I hugged them all, one after another, I was aware that, somewhere in this enormous crowd were the others—the few hundred Jews who had come down from the mountains, from their hiding-places in caves and Roman ruins, from the monasteries and private houses of Assisi, to celebrate the joyful day of their liberation.

A jeep drove into the square to pick up the Lieutenant. I heard the officer ask, 'Where is Villa Fortini?' A few boys jumped on the vehicle, all eager to guide him. It was at the Villa Fortini that Lieutenant Garigue was setting up his Military Headquarters. I smiled to myself, wondering how long it would take Fortini to enrol the British Town Commandant as a member of the International Society for Franciscan Studies.

The bells continued to peal, uninterruptedly. My brothers and I made our way to the Basilica of St Francis to sing our grateful Te Deum at the tomb of our holy saint. But as we were almost at the entrance, we heard not only the sound of bells but, surprisingly, also of music. Quickly, I ran up the stairs into the Basilica. There, at the huge organ, at the other end of an aisle, sat the monk with his artistic white mop of hair—Maestro Fano. He was not playing a Gregorian chant, or St Francis's Canticle of the Creatures or even the Te Deum. The Basilica's loudspeakers were carrying through the town and even further, into the surrounding Umbrian countryside, the majestic and beautiful chords of God Save the King.

Epilogue by Alexander Ramati

I heard those surging, triumphant notes mingling with the music of church bells reverberating all over the city of Assisi. Together with a few other Allied war correspondents, I was in a jeep driving into the city on 17 June 1944, right on the heels of the conquering troops. We also tasted the applause, the flowers, the wine and the embraces as we inched our way through the crowd to the Piazza del Comune. There, a huge, printed banner, spanning the road at the entrance to the Via Paolo, caught my attention. It was stuck over the familiar Fascist one featuring Mussolini saying 'I'm advancing. Follow me!' The banner read, 'The Jews of Italy have Italian blood, Italian souls and Italian genius. Mazzini.'

I asked the driver to stop. My companions, a British, an American and a French correspondent, alighted from the car, too, and went straight to the Café Excelsior. Fascinated, I walked up to the banner. Some of the local people were standing in front of it.

'What does it mean?' I asked an imposingly tall, moustached man. 'And why Jews?'

'A few hundred of them were saved here,' he answered.

I still remember how my heart leapt. I was not just a correspondent covering the war. I was a soldier of the Second Polish Corps of General Anders, part of General Montgomery's British Eighth Army, and I was writing for our army newspaper. We had taken Monte Cassino and now our corps was being transferred to the Adriatic coast to advance towards Ancona. I was a Pole, but I was also a Jew. My parents and younger brother had remained in Brest Litovsk under the Nazis, and, I hoped, on that day were already under the Russians. That is if they were alive. It was here, in Assisi, that for the first time I was about to see some European Jews safe and alive. I remember raising my eyes to the sky—I was young and trusted in God—and praying for my family. On my way from Brest Litovsk, via Russia and the Middle East, I had come to Palestine and there, in Jerusalem, I had, like many other Jewish soldiers, placed a letter to God in a crevice of the Wailing Wall, and in it I had asked that my family survive the war. If there were good men in Assisi, perhaps there were some, too, in Brest Litovsk, though painfully I knew the difference. In my home town there were as many Jews as in the whole of Italy.

The tall man, seeing my red armband with the English words 'War Correspondent', introduced himself. 'I am Giovanni Cardelli,' he said.

'Who wrote that sign?' I asked.

'Luigi Brizi,' he said. 'An anti-Fascist, a printer who helped to make false papers for Jewish refugees, and a descendant of a former Mayor of Assisi who was a supporter of Mazzini.'

'And where are those Jews?'

The man waved his hand in a circular motion. 'All over the town, celebrating together with us.'

'Who saved them?'

'We did,' he said. 'We who were part of the city's underground, the Italians who took them into their homes, but most of all the monks and the nuns, and the Bishop, and Don Brunacci and Padre Niccacci—most of all Padre Niccacci.'

'I would like to meet him.' I said.

And that was how I met Padre Rufino Salvatore Niccacci. Not far from where I stood. He had already made his way to the Café Minerva to join Brizi, attired in his festive black borsalino. They were both drinking the diluted Umbrian wine, hoping that soon it would become undiluted. And it was here that I first heard the story of what happened in Assisi between September 1943 and June 1944.

I was twenty-three and, like most journalists, I wanted to write a book one day. Assisi was the first Italian town in which I took no interest in the lovely signorine offering wine and inviting everyone home for a meal. I was interested in Padre Rufino and in being introduced to the people he had helped to save. The Padre took me to meet many of the Jews and many of those who had hidden them, including Bishop Nicolini. And then, before leaving Assisi, I told the Padre that one day, soon, I would come back to write their story. He did not ask me to; no one there wanted praises to be sung for their acts of human charity. It was I who made that vow to myself. What I did not know at the time was that more than thirty years would pass before I would be able to keep that promise.

My parents and brother did survive the war—three of sixteen, out of the 40,000 Jews, who had been hidden by Gentiles, Dziunia and Stanislaw Leparski. And so I wrote my first book about them. Other books followed—about my family, relatives, neighbours, Polish Jews—about *my* holocaust and my country of birth, and then about how they were rebuilding their life in their real country, in Israel, where finally they were safe and where there would never be another holocaust. But I never forgot that promise to Father Niccacci, not because I had made it and wanted to keep my word but because I felt guilty at not bringing to life a splendid record of a wonderful Christian city. Assisi had saved three hundred Jews, and many times that number if one counts the documents produced and delivered to survivors in other towns. And that record was so much greater because it was a city where no Jew had ever lived before. It was a city that had saved strangers. And by now that guilt cried out in me, because three decades later it was already a forgotten episode in the increasingly forgotten holocaust of the Second World War.

In the summer of 1972, while in Holland, I placed a long-distance telephone call to San Damiano. The monk who answered it had never heard of Padre Rufino. I phoned the Basilica of St Francis. No one there knew who he was. Only when I reached the Bishop's Palace was I told that they would inquire of his whereabouts. The next day I was given his address by the Monsignore's niece: c/o I Frati Minori, presso parrocchia di Pontenuovo di Deruta. I did not write; I telephoned the only number listed in the village of Pontenuovo, the public phone booth. A passer-by who answered it took it upon himself to see to it that Padre Rufino would await my call the following day at 10 a.m.

He remembered. He had always had an excellent memory. I told him that I would be coming to Pontenuovo in a few days' time. He said I would find him in the parish church. He had a room above the church. When I arrived there with my wife and daughter, I went straight to the church, its benches packed with local inhabitants. White-robed choirboys were helping the priest celebrate mass. Then I recognised the priest. Padre Rufino was bald now, but the same burning light shone under bushy brows in his brown eyes. I sat there, deeply moved, listening to his paters and aves, my thoughts going back to those other Jews sitting in their monks' habits in San Damiano, attending his service. When he had finished, I walked into the sacristy and as he was taking off and folding his chasuble and alb, revealing beneath them his Franciscan habit, he looked up at me. We embraced each other the way both Italians and Poles do. 'I am sorry for the delay,' I smiled, 'but here I am, ready to start.'

The research began with lunch. A big lunch, one kilometre away, at Via Molinella, Deruta, where the family mill was now being run by Vincenzo and Alberto, the sons of Luigi. After we had sampled Umbrian salami and drunk robust red, undiluted country wine, their mother, Maria, now full and matronly with an amiable smile, brought her faraoni, which Alberto had shot for the meal. We sat at the table, my wife and two-year old daughter, where once another Slav Jew, Finzi, had sat with his wife and two-year old Brigitte, before their son was born, and where the three Niccacci brothers had fêted the man about to be taken away by the Fascist police. Only one of the three was still alive, Padre Rufino, and during that long sumptuous meal he told me in great detail of what had happened to some of the refugees and the people who had saved them, including himself, in the time between my two visits to the Assisi region.

Shortly after the town's liberation, a soldier of the Palestine Brigade, Corporal Yehuda Hirsh, arrived, going from monastery to monastery, asking whether there were any Jews there. At San Quirico, where the Gelbs were staying once more, the youngest of the three sisters, Hanna, had opened the door for him. Within a day, he had gathered a dozen of his army friends and brought them to Assisi. A party, attended by Jewish soldiers, Jewish refugees, monks, extern nuns and clergymen, was arranged immediately in the big courtyard of the Hermitage, on Mount Subasio. It was also the beginning of the courtship of Hanna by Corporal Hirsh.

All the children attending the school received new certificates under their real names, in lieu of those given them under false ones; not one school year was lost. The cross over Clara Bianchi's grave was replaced by the Star of David and her name changed back to Clara Weiss; today it is still the only Jewish tombstone in the Catholic cemetery of Assisi. All the engaged couples got married; George married Hella, Pali married Deborah, Yehuda married Hanna and Dr Carlo Maionica married Franca Covarelli. Giovanni Cardelli, the anti-Fascist leader, became the new Mayor of the town, and in Florence one of the wartime underground associates of Cardinal della Costa, Giorgio La Pira, became Mayor. The former Mayor of Assisi, Arnaldo Fortini, was sent by the British to an internment camp, but after six weeks he returned to his city, to write several more books on St Francis and to continue to preside over the work of the International Society for Franciscan Studies. For his lifetime's devotion to propagating St Francis's message of 'Pax et Bonum' and for his untiring efforts to end wars, he was nominated by Italy for the Nobel Peace Prize, alas without success.

Also unsuccessful was Colonel Müller's noble effort to leave to the city the expensive medical supplies, at the risk of prosecution by the German military authorities. The British confiscated the stock as a war trophy and took it all away, leaving a token portion for the town. The two anti-Fascists, Colonel Paolo Gay and Lieutenant Antonio Podda, were liberated by the Allies from Perugia jail. Gay retired to Torino, Podda became personal pilot to the Italian President, Luigi Einaudi.

With the end of the war, most of the refugees returned home, the Finzis to their distant one, in Antwerp; some left for Palestine, but one family, enamoured of the people who had offered them hospitality at the peril of their own lives, the Viterbis, remained in their apartment in Renato Carli's house on Borgo Aretino—the first Jewish family ever to settle in Assisi. Many of those who left and prospered were anxious to express their gratitude. They gave generously to the poor, donated funds to Bishop Nicolini for his charitable work and presented Luigi Brizi with a brand-new, modern printing press.

Colonel Valentin Müller kept his promise. He returned to

Assisi in September 1950, bringing with him his wife, his son Robert and daughter Irmgard, both already studying medicine. When the word spread that the Colonello was staying at the Hotel Subasio, the townspeople came out to welcome him, forcing him to appear on the balcony. Gifts and flowers were left for him and Signor and Signora Rossi invited him and his family to stay as long as they wished as their guests. The Bishop invited them to a party, and the town's Communist Mayor, Dr Sebastiano Veneziano, held a reception for the Colonel. There was a proposal to erect a monument in his honour, but it was agreed that a street should be named after him; by law this could only be done twenty years after his death. It never happened. The administration changed; the idea was forgotten and abandoned.

Colonel Müller of course met Padre Niccacci—this time walking to San Damiano with his family. He attended mass and then had a cheerful reunion with other brothers and fathers taking part. At one point the Colonel asked, 'And where is the Father that composed the beautiful music for St Francis's "Canticle to the Creatures"?' There was the hint of a smile in his eyes and Padre Rufino thought that the Colonel perhaps had known all along about the Jews hidden in Assisi. He did not ask Müller; if he had managed to deceive him, he did not want to gloat over it. Ten months after his visit to Assisi, Colonel Müller died of a brain tumour at the age of sixty.

In 1955, the Jewish Community of Italy, on the tenth anniversary of the ending of the war, issued gold medals to those Christians who had made a great contribution to the rescue of the Italian Jews. In Assisi they were presented to Bishop Nicolini, Fathers Niccacci and Todde, Don Brunacci, Mother Giuseppina and Luigi Brizi, the latter accepted by Trento on behalf of his late father. One medal recipient, in Perugia, just missed its delivery by a few hours. Don Federico Vincenti, of the San Andrea Church, a refuge and relay station to Assisi, had just passed away. One of the protagonists of the rescue operation received a different kind of award, the one he wanted more than anything else. Gino Battaglia, the cyclist-courier, won the Tour de France after the war, beating his much younger rivals.

Many of the Jewish survivors, including the Kropfs and the Gelbs, came that year to Assisi for a reunion. Again a party was held at the Hermitage. Two years later, Padre Niccacci was transferred to the nearby town of Trevi and placed in charge of a Catholic orphanage of two hundred boys attached to the monastery of San Martino. And a great part of his funds came from grateful survivors. For those Jews whose lives had been saved, just like their Christian benefactors, were imbued with the idea that we are all our brother's keepers.

Father Rufino took me to the Bishop, to Don Brunacci, Mother Giuseppina and the others. I spent a month in Assisi, researching. On several occasions I visited the Bishop, by then already ninety-five years old, and listened to his account of the wartime events and shared with him at least half a dozen bottles of Santa Giustina wine, from the stock that he replenished immediately after the war. He granted me access to his library and his papers. Gemma Fortini showed me her late father's office, left with pen in the inkpot, his appointment diary and a notebook on his desk, just as if he were to return there any moment. The walls were lined not only with his books, but also with folders filled with newspaper clippings and all the documents meticulously collected during his entire tenure of office as the city's Mayor and President of the International Society for Franciscan Studies. I spoke to Trento Brizi, Giovanni Cardelli, Signora Violante Rossi, the Viterbis, and of course to Don Brunacci. And then I interviewed others—monks, nuns, priests, former underground members and former Fascist leaders.

From Assisi I travelled to Perugia, Rome, Florence, Milan and Trieste. It was in Trieste that I gathered a wealth of information and a score of Brizi-forged documents from the Gelbs, the Kropfs, the Maionicas and the Klugmans. In Israel I saw a number of people who had settled there. Not only old Baruch who, like Nicolini, died at the age of ninety-six, but Hanna Hirsh, formerly Gelb, her three cousins, Mira, Hella and Lea, and also Baruch's granddaughters, who, together with their parents Marco and Herminia, were sheltered in the Convent of Stigmata. I also met a few families such as that of Dr Julius Scheib, who hid in private homes, their true identity known only to Padre Rufino and to Luigi Brizi. In Nazareth I met Professor Emanuele Testa of Rome's Pontifical College, who was a young seminarist at the Basilica of Santa Maria degli Angeli and whose sister perished in Foligno. Finally, I travelled to Eichstätt. At 14 Leopoldstrasse, the home and clinic of Dr Robert Müller, both of which he had inherited from his father, I spent a few days examining the Colonel's papers. And then, together with his son, I visited the tomb of Dr Müller. His name was inscribed above the relief map of his beloved city of Assisi and the Latin motto *In serviendo consumor*. And it was in this ancient, small Bavarian town that I asked the son the question that Padre Rufino had not dared to ask his father. Did Colonel Müller know that hundreds of Jews were being hidden in Assisi? 'He suspected it,' the son answered; and then he added, 'and if he was deceived by the Italian underground, it is because he wanted to be deceived.'

In April 1974, I received a letter from Padre Niccacci. He was fulfilling his lifelong dream of finally saving enough money to be able to make a pilgrimage to the Holy Land. I met him at the airport. Security-conscious officials made him open his battered suitcase. He smiled at me. This was not the OVRA and he was not smuggling documents. But he had no idea of the reception awaiting him. Notified of his visit, the Yad Vashem, Israel's Memorial Authority, who for the past twenty-one years had collected and preserved the records of six million Jews murdered by the Nazis as well as of those Gentiles who had risked their lives to save Jews, had arranged a ceremony to honour the poor peasant monk who became the hero of a wartime rescue operation. A forgotten hero. His file was only number 876, and he was only the 300th person to be honoured in Israel and only the twenty-fifth Italian. For, in spite of their love for the dramatic, the Italians showed great restraint in telling of their actions which had resulted in saving 80 per cent of Italian Jewry, the opposite of what happened in the rest of Europe, where, except for Denmark with its 8,000 Jews spirited away to Sweden, 80 per cent of the Jews perished. All in all, 32,000 Italian Jews and several thousand foreign Jews were hidden successfully by the Italian people, most of them in monasteries and religious institutions. Monsignore Montini, who headed the Holy See's Aid Service to Refugees during the war, and who in 1955 was to become a Cardinal and later Pope Paul VI, turned down the gold medal offered him by the Jewish Community of Italy. 'I acted in the line of duty,' he answered, 'and for that I am not entitled to a medal.'

On 29 April 1974, I stood in the Avenue of the Righteous Gentiles together with government officials, refugees saved by Padre Rufino and the Franciscan dignitaries who are the Holy See's custodians of the Holy Land. I watched the friar, now sixty-three, take a shovel, dig a hole, plant a carob tree sapling and water it. A plaque bearing his name in both Latin and Hebrew letters was placed beside it.

We then all went to the Memorial Hall, in front of which stood the sculpture of a praying but defiant Job, his fist clenched, demanding an answer from heaven. In the dark hall the eternal flame was burning. The black marble floor only had names engraved on it: Auschwitz, Treblinka, Chelmno, Dachau, Buchenwald, Bergen-Belsen, Mauthausen, Babi Yar—more than twenty stations to the Jewish people's Golgotha. There, as the military guard stood to attention and the children gathered around, the friar was flanked by the people he had saved and the cantor intoned the solemn Hebrew chants. The prayers over, the representative of the government presented the medal and the diploma of the Righteous Gentile, the highest honour Israel can bestow on a Christian, to Padre Rufino Salvatore Niccacci.

After the Padre had made his tour of the Christian holy places, I became his guide to the Jewish ones and to modern Israel. Then I brought him to my home. It was here, after dinner, that I told him what had been on my mind for a long time—that in order to tell the story as truthfully and as vividly as possible, he ought to narrate it himself. My research of other sources confirmed everything he had told me. He had an excellent memory of the events and I could easily help him by bringing some details to his attention.

Padre Niccacci was taken aback. He was good at delivering sermons, but he was not a writer. I managed to persuade him to stay with me for several weeks. In great detail he described the events that had taken place more than thirty years before. And that is how this book was born—part of it written while he was still in Israel, parts of it sent to him in Deruta for further approval. It has come out, I hope, as if it were written by Padre Niccacci himself—if he were a writer. As for me, it grew out of my need as a Jew to pay gratitude to a Gentile, to all Gentiles who were not afraid to lose their own lives to save the lives of others.

Last summer I came to Deruta with the final portion of the book. I was told at the Pontenuovo church that I would find the friar at the top of Montenero. It was there, I recalled, that he used to play as a child with his brothers Luigi and Enrico. After half an hour's steep climb, I reached the mountain top. And there I saw Padre Rufino, his nephews Vincenzo and Alberto and a few other relatives, planting saplings along the freshly gravelled roads. As usual he embraced me effusively, and pointed with pride to his new achievement. He had managed to cajole the Italian government into leasing him Montenero, free of charge. Together with his family he had built access roads and was about to complete the planting of trees, not just one, as in Jerusalem's Avenue of the Righteous Gentiles, but ten thousand of them, along several avenues that were to become the streets of a small settlement housing destitute Christian and Jewish families, and in its very centre, an Ecumenical House, to which Christians and Jews could come from all over the world to discuss the problems of greater rapprochement between Christianity and Judaism. Of course he needed funds for the project, but bursting with tireless energy and optimism, undiminished by age, he had no doubt that they would come in time. I have no doubt either. Padre Rufino Niccacci was entitled to see his project come alive. After all, he had started his own ecumenical dialogue with the Jews a whole decade before Pope John XXIII.

Some time after this book had already gone to the printer, Don Aldo Brunacci came to Jerusalem with a group of Assisi pilgrims, to commemorate the 750th anniversary of St Francis' death. He was the bearer of the sad news that Padre Rufino Niccacci had died.

Don Aldo and the late Bishop Nicolini were honoured, too, by the government of Israel with the medals and titles of the Righteous Gentile. Assisi's new bishop, Dino Tomassini, received the award on behalf of his predecessor. Again the ceremony was attended by Jewish war-time refugees in Assisi who were now living in Israel.

After planting his carob tree sapling, Don Aldo said, 'Let us pay our respects to Padre Rufino'. We were led to another carob tree, a bigger one, three years old, marked with a plaque 'Padre Rufino Niccacci'. Don Aldo folded his hands: 'Dominus pascit me...', he began. And as he and the new Bishop of Assisi, the Vatican's minister plenipotentiary and the Italian consul-general intoned 'The Lord is my shepherd' in Latin, the Hebrew voices of the Jewish survivors, rescued by Padre Rufino from the holocaust, joined them in reciting David's Psalm for the dead. I could not help but think of that distant time when, before embarking on his very first mission, Padre Rufino and his brothers and the Jews he was to take to safety, prayed together in the Basilica of Santa Maria degli Angeli.

Later I was told by Don Aldo that Padre Rufino, who died in November 1977 at the young age of 66, worked till the very last on his project of the Ecumenical House. To the memory of this noble peasant and the most righteous gentile it has been my privilege to know, this book is dedicated.

For Product Safety Concerns and Information please contact our EU
representative GPSR@taylorandfrancis.com
Taylor & Francis Verlag GmbH, Kaufingerstraße 24, 80331 München, Germany

www.ingramcontent.com/pod-product-compliance
Lightning Source LLC
Chambersburg PA
CBHW070614300426
44113CB00010B/1520